JENNY ERICKSON

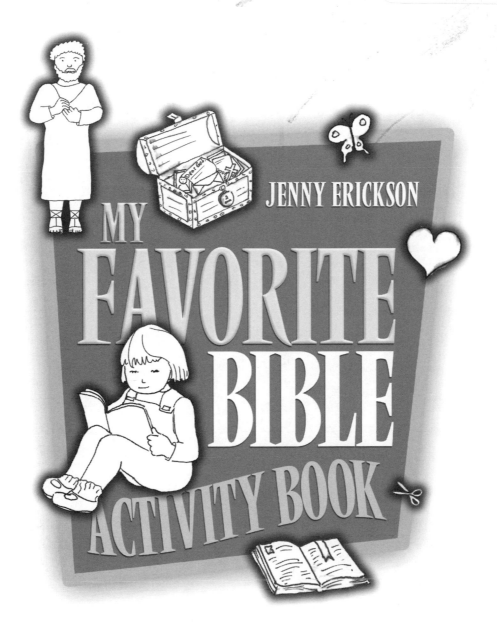

MY FAVORITE BIBLE ACTIVITY BOOK

TWENTY-THIRD PUBLICATIONS
185 WILLOW STREET • PO BOX 180 • MYSTIC, CT 06355
TEL: 1-800-321-0411 • FAX: 1-800-572-0788
E-MAIL: ttpubs@aol.com • www.twentythirdpublications.com
Bayard

Dedication

To my Dad
Thank you for your encouragement,
laughter, and wisdom.

And to my Mom
Who has gone beyond the stars—
You will always be in my heart.
With love, #4

The Scripture passages contained herein are from the *New Revised Standard Version of the Bible*, copyright© 1989, by the Division of Christian Education of the National Council of Churches in the U.S.A. All rights reserved.

Twenty-Third Publications
A Division of Bayard
185 Willow Street
P.O. Box 180
Mystic, CT 06355
(860) 536-2611 or (800) 321-0411
www.twentythirdpublications.com
ISBN:1-58595-268-0

Printed in the U.S.A.

Contents

May

Introduction

Within me there is something like a burning fire shut up in my bones;
I am weary with holding it in, and I cannot.
—Jeremiah 20:9

When I was about ten years old, I told my parents that I was going to read the Bible—from cover to cover. It was a good resolution, but hard to keep. The long names and the battles the Israelites fought were too difficult for me to get through, and soon the Bible was back on the shelf.

Years later, my old resolution resurfaced and became the inspiration for this book. As much as possible, I have tried to recapture and to simplify some of the favorite Old Testament narratives. To engage the children in the learning process, I do this through a variety of activities: crosswords, word searches, mazes, cryptoquips, hidden pictures, drawings, and more.

My Favorite Bible Activity Book follows a September through May format, with several activities per month. Any of these can be used throughout the year, however, for a wide range of purposes. For example, you might want to use a section of the book as the basis for a Vacation Bible School. Or, you can adapt several activities for family catechetical gatherings during the year. The possibilities for use are limitless.

It would be helpful for you to have a Bible available when you work with the children on these activities, so that if any questions arise you can refer to the original source. Please be aware that the wording in your translation may be different from the wording in this book.

As you teach, you may be inspired to read the actual accounts in the Bible to discover interesting details about the various stories. Encourage the children to read from the Bible as well, whether from an adult edition, or from one of the many children's versions that are available, some of which are listed in the resource section at the back of this book. It would be helpful to have all materials at hand before you actually do the projects with your children. This will facilitate the process, especially if you are working with a large number of children.

As a journeying people towards God, we know our roots, we love our salvation history. As teachers of God's word, we do as our spiritual forefathers: we pass on the torch!

September Prayer

Bless me,

O God.

During this new school year

I want to work hard

so that I may learn many things.

Help me to understand your holy Word

and grant that I will grow every day

in your love.

Amen.

God's Letter to Us

Did you ever get a card or letter in the mail? Isn't it fun to open up the envelope and see what is inside?

God has written a special letter to you, too. Do you know what this letter to you is called? Find the answer in the puzzle below. Spell out the names of each picture. What word remains in the squares?

The Bible is God's letter to you! In the Bible, you will read about God's chosen people and how they lived. You will find heroes to imitate and prayers to say.

In the Bible, you will meet Jesus, the Son of God. Your heart will be glad when you hear what Jesus did and what he had to say! In the Bible you can read about the early Christians and the adventures they had.

God tells you in his letter how much he loves you and cares for you.

Did you know that at any time you can write a letter to God? In your letter, tell God about:

• how you feel
• people you know
• things you like or don't like
• how you want to know God better
• anything!

When you are done, you won't need to mail your letter. Just keep it in a special notebook or box. As you know, God is always near you and can see whatever you write.

Your letter to God is your very own, personal, written prayer.

Now write a short letter to God using the next page as your stationery.

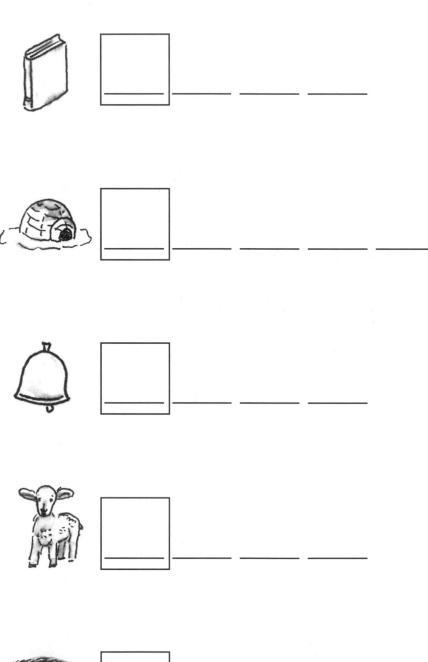

A Treasure for You

Have you ever been on a treasure hunt? What did you find?

A treasure map is a map that can lead someone to buried treasure. God has a treasure for you. To find it, look at the treasure map on this page and follow the directions in order. What is the treasure?

Directions:

"N" stands for up North; S stands for down South; W stands for out West; and E stands for back East.

Start at the letter "G"; write this on the line   **G**

Go North ⬆ one letter; write this on the line: _____

Go West ⬅ two letters; write this on the line: _____

Go East ➡ one letter; write this on the line: _____

Go South ⬇ two letters; write this on the line: _____

Go West ⬅ one letter; write this on the line: _____

Go South ⬇ one letter; write this on the line: _____

Go East ➡ two letters; write this on the line: _____

Circle the picture below the last letter.

Now you can make your own treasure box! Look at the next two pages for directions.

D	S	O
L	P	G
O	W	M
R	B	D

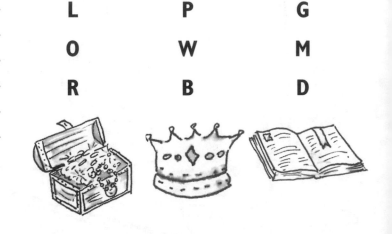

What is God's treasure for you?

Make a Treasure Box

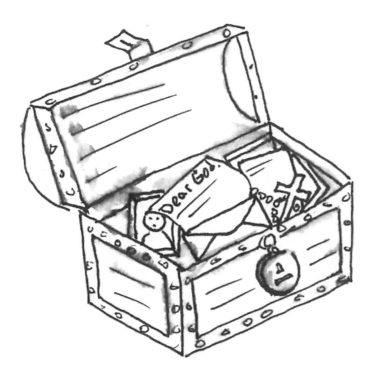

What you need :
A shoe box with cover, construction paper, glue, markers, stickers

What you do:
Ask an adult to help you. Cut the construction paper to the size of the box; glue it well to the box. With markers, write on it "My Treasure Box." Add any stickers you may have or cut out and use the pictures on the next page to decorate your box. Be creative!

Finally, cut out the poem below and glue it to the inside cover of your treasure box.

Items to put in your treasure box: your favorite Bible quotes, prayers, letters you write to God, holy cards, holy pictures, religious articles like a cross, rosary, pin, photos of people who are special to you.

God gave me one life to live; I'll do my very best
to live my life on earth with love and faith and zest.

God listens to my prayer, and sees my kindness and patience, too.
I always try to obey God's will in what I say and do.

I'll take the time to read God's Word, to pray and grow in grace;
I will look forward to the day when I will see God's face.

In this box I'll keep the treasures I pick up along the way
these things will help me remember God each and every day.

My greatest treasure is the Lord; this I surely understand
and I'll be glad that I have served God well when I reach the Promised Land.

My Treasure Box

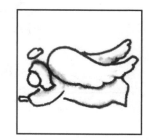

The Word of God

Read the sentences below. Then find the underlined words in the word search. You can look across, diagonally, up, down, and backwards.

```
C P W I S D O M D A G
B H O L Y B O O K G O
E E R U T P I R C S S
C O D W A L F B D K P
A L E T T E R Q L Y E
R N M Z Y A R P O E L
G L I S T E N P S L N
```

It is important to <u>pray</u> before reading God's Word.

Other words or phrases we use for <u>Bible</u> are <u>Holy Book</u>, <u>Scripture</u>, God's <u>Word</u>.

The two main parts of the Bible are the <u>Old</u> and the <u>New</u> Testaments.

The Bible is God's <u>letter</u> to us.

The Bible teaches us God's <u>law</u>.

The <u>Gospel</u> includes the books of Matthew, Mark, Luke, and John in the New Testament.

The Gospel tells us about the life of Jesus and what he taught.

During Mass every Sunday we <u>listen</u> closely to the reading of Scripture.

The Bible has many lessons about growing in <u>wisdom</u> and <u>grace</u>.

(You will need to have at least one copy of the Bible available; if possible, have one for all the children.)

You can learn how to find your way through the Bible all by yourself! First, open up a Bible. Look through the first few pages and find the Contents page. The Old Testament and the New Testament are listed separately, because each has its own list of *books*.

Finding Your Way in the Bible

On the Contents page, the number after each book is the number of the page you can turn to in the Bible to find that book.

1. Look down the list to the book of Ruth. What page is it on? Turn to that page.

2. Now flip through the pages. The bigger numbers indicate the chapter of the book. Count the chapters to the end of the book of Ruth. How many chapters are there? _____

3. Now look at the words of the story. Can you see the tiny numbers in between the text? (Some Bibles have numbers going down the left or right sides of the page.) Those numbers point out what verse you are reading.

4. Go to the contents page again. Find the book of Genesis. How would you look up this reference? First, you would turn to the book of Genesis, then look for chapter fourteen and go through the story until you come to verse eighteen.

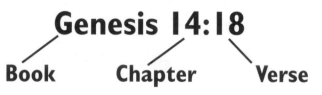

Genesis 14:18

Book   **Chapter**   **Verse**

5. After reading the passage above, you will be able to finish the following sentence:

   Melchizadek, the king of Salem, was a priest of God; before he blessed Abram, Melchizadek brought out _____ and _____.

6. Try another quote (or reference). Find Genesis 7:13. What are the names of Noah's sons? Write them here:

   _____

Congratulations! You are on the way to discovering how to read the Bible!

Make a Bookmark

Here is a bookmark you can make for your Bible.

What you need:
Crayons, markers, scissors, clear wide tape, hole punch, yarn cut into 6 inch strands

Here's what to do:

1 Color the bookmark and cut it out. Or, you can trace or copy this page, then color and cut out bookmark.

2 Get clear contact paper or clear packing tape and seal your finished bookmark. This will make it stronger and keep it from getting smudged.

3 With a hole punch, make a hole at the top of the bookmark.

4 Take three six-inch strands of yarn and push them through the hole. Now double knot the ends firmly against the bookmark. Trim any uneven strands. Now you have a tassel on your bookmark!

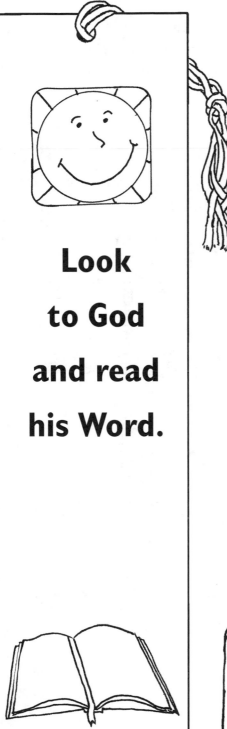

**Look
to God
and read
his Word.**

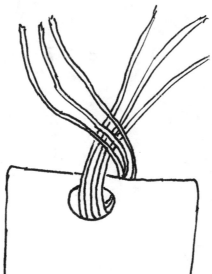

When your great, great-grandparents were children, they did not have electricity in their house. They had to use oil lamps and candles just to read a book or do their homework. In order for them to find their way around the house at night, they had to carry an oil lamp or candle around with them. Since Thomas Edison invented the light bulb, however, no one has to do that anymore.

There might be some times in your life when you aren't sure what choices to make. When some people experience that kind of uncertainty, they say they are "in the dark." They just don't know what to do and can't see the way through their difficulties.

But God doesn't want you to ever feel alone and in the dark. He gave you something very important to light up your way. Can you guess what it is? It is the Bible.

God Guides Us

Here is a short prayer that you can pray. It is found in Psalm 119:105. First figure out the prayer with the clues of the cryptoquip. Then turn to this passage of the Bible and read more of this psalm.

1 = A	4 = F	7 = I	10 = N	13 = R	16 = U
2 = D	5 = G	8 = L	11 = O	14 = S	17 = W
3 = E	6 = H	9 = M	12 = P	15 = T	18 = Y

___ ___ ___ ___   ___ ___ ___ ___
18 11 16 13   17 11 13   2

___ ___ ___   ___ ___ ___ ___
7 14   1   8   1   9 12

___ ___ ___   ___ ___   ___ ___ ___ ___
4 11 13   9 18   4   3   3 15

___   ___ ___ ___ ___ ___ ___   ___ ___
1   8   7   5   6 15   11 10

___ ___ ___ ___ ___ ___
9 18 12   1 15   6

Creature Feature

Did you ever wonder what kinds of animals and reptiles lived in Bible times? Here is a crossword of creatures mentioned in Scripture. Most of the ones here are very familiar. The reference below each one tells you where to find the animal in the Bible. Spell out the creature's name in the crossword. A few are done for you.

Crossword entries filled in:

3. MULE
6. TURTLEDOVE
10. WEASEL
16. SPARROW
17. (down) RAVEN
26. (down) RABBIT
30. BIRD

Down

2. Lev 11:29
4. Jer 5:6
7. Ex 12:3
8. Is 7:21
11. Prov 23:5
12. Zec 1:8
13. Deut 14:5
15. Mt 18:12
17. Lev 11:15
18. Is 11:6
20. Prov 30:31
22. Lk 2:24
24. Job 39:26
26. Deut 14:7
29. Lk 15:16

Across

1. Gen 24:64
3. Zec 14:15
6. Jer 8:7
8. Mt 23:37
9. Is 11:7
10. Lev 11:29
13. Mt 15:27
14. Dan 6:27
15. Is 3:1
16. Mt 10:31
19. Jer 8:7
21. Lk 14:5
23. Mt 12:40
25. Ps 105:30
27. Mt 14:17
28. Lev 11:17
30. Gen 1:22
31. Mt 25:32

13

Make a Bible Jar

Every day things happen—good things, bad things, anything. Sometimes we can't understand why something happened. Sometimes we might even feel so frustrated that we just want to yell, "Help me Lord!" You know what? Even if you whispered it, God would hear you! Just take the time to "listen" to what he has to say.

Here is an activity you can do to help you listen to God. Make a Bible jar and fill it with references from the Bible. At least once a week, or even more often, reach in and take out a slip of paper. Find the quote in the Bible that is written on that piece of paper. Read it, sit quietly for a few minutes, and listen to what God has to say. See if you can memorize the Scripture passage you chose.

What you need:

Glue, construction paper, scissors, crayons, markers, or colored pencils, a wide-mouthed container, for example, an empty coffee can or a round empty oatmeal container (the opening should be wide enough for you to get your hand in and out of the container).

Note: Use the abbreviated key in your Bible to help you with the abbreviated names of the Bible books.

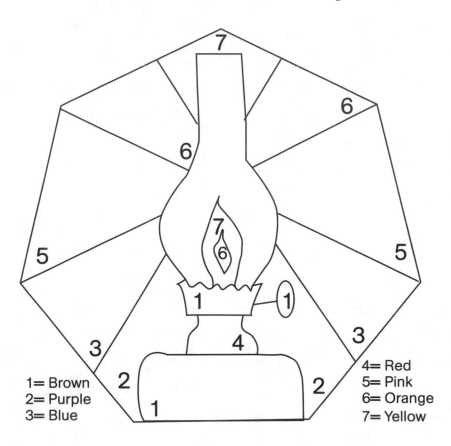

1= Brown
2= Purple
3= Blue
4= Red
5= Pink
6= Orange
7= Yellow

What to do:

Glue construction paper to the outside of the container.

1. Color the picture below, cut it out, and glue it to a piece of construction paper. (You can also trace or copy the drawing, then color and cut it out.)

2. Write the passage from Psalm 119:105 somewhere on the construction paper, either above or below the lamp.

3. Glue the construction paper to the outside of the jar.

4. Make enough copies of the biblical references on the following two pages so that each child may have a set. Then cut out the references on the following pages to put inside the Bible jar. Note to the teacher/parent: To save time, use a paper cutter to cut the citations out ahead of time. Don't forget to have a copy of the abbreviation key found in the appendix of this book).

Note to parent/teacher: To save time, use a "one-knife" or paper cutter to cut straight rows prior to the lesson, thus making it easier for the children. Use the key to abbreviations in the front of your Bible if you need help.

Ps 62:1	Zec 8:16	Lk 1:37	Mt 5:7	Ps 23:4	Jas 1:12
Jn 20:29	Col 3:20	Jn 14:2	Rv 3:20	Mt 5:8	Dt 7:9
2 Thes 3:3	Ps 34:19	Is 40:30	Rv 21:7	Is 60:20	Jer 33:3
Sir 28:2	Ps 46:1	Ex 33:14	Gal 6:9	Lk 6:36	Jas 5:13
Mt 5:3	Lk 18:14	Jb 23:10	I Pt 5:7	I Pt 3:12	Prv 28:7
Sir 27:8	Rom 12:12	Mt 5:6	Prv 3:3	Lk 6:37	Jos 1:9
Gal 2:20	Ps 50:15	Ps 103:12	Prv 1:8	Rv 21:4	Is 30:18
Prv 18:15	Mt 5:5	Acts 2:21	I Jn 3:18	Jas 4:10	2 Cor 12:9
Mt 5:4	Mk 8:35	Rom 8:28	Is 40:31	Mt 5:9	Jas 4:8

Jn 15:9	Mt 7:7	1 Jn 2:17	Jn 10:27	Jn 14:15	Mt 25:40
Jn 6:35	Mt 4:19	Jn 14:15	Ps 103:11	Jn 6:48–51	Acts 17:28
Mk 8:35	Mt 10:42	Jn 14:13	Ps 34:18	Ps 51:10	Mt 28:20
Mt 5:10	Lk 6:23	Mt 11:28	Ps 37:5	Jn 6:54–55	Tb 14:8
Lk 6:38	Jn 14:27	Mt 18:19	Phil 1:27	Ps 27:1	Mt 5:16
Mk 8:37	Prv 21:23	Mt 24:35	Sir 7:30	Ps 37:8	Mt 22:37
Ps 16:8	Ps 34:17	Prv 3:6	Lv 26:11–12	Jn 19:25–27	Prv 15:32
Prv 3:12	Rom 4:8	Ps 16:11	Prv 27:2	Ps 27:14	Tb 4:21
Jn 12:26	Gal 6:22–23	Mt 18:20	1 Cor 13:13	Heb 13:5–6	Mt 22:38
Jn 12:46	Ps 50:14	Mt 21:22	Mk 10:14	Acts 20:35	Mt 11:28–29

October Prayer

Lord,

You want me to enjoy

all the beauty of Autumn,

For this I pray,

Blessed be God, my Creator!

You want me to see your face

in the different people

you created around me.

For this I pray,

Blessed be God, my Creator!

You love me for who I am

and you call me to be an important part

of your plan in salvation history.

For all these things, I pray,

Blessed be God, my Creator!

To Parents and Catechists:

With the arrival of Autumn and nature's panorama of colors, the children can relate well to the stories of creation. Perhaps use a walk outdoors during class to open conversation about God's handiwork. The changing season provides an analogy of God's salvific plan: although Fall and Winter signify a type of death and darkness, there is always Spring to hope for! Similarly, Adam and Eve, Cain and Abel, and most of the other Old Testament figures struggled with sin—just as we do. But through promises, covenants, and forgiveness, God offers us a way out of the darkness of sin and into the light of salvation.

In the beginning, God created the world. God made the sun and the moon and the stars, the oceans and lakes and all the creatures that live in the water. God made the land and the trees and all the animals that live on the land. Then God made Adam and Eve, the first humans.

God was happy with everything he created! He even made a really beautiful place for Adam and Eve to live. It was called "The Garden of Eden."

Everything God made has a purpose. We have a purpose too! God wants to be known and loved and served, and given glory. And at least once a week we should go to church to worship God, our loving Creator.

Creation
Gen 1:2

Circle the pictures of the things Adam and Eve may have seen in the garden.

Make your own prayer of praise by filling in the blanks.

I Praise You, God!

Dear God,

I am glad you created _____.

I praise you for the things I see in nature, like _____.

When I look at them, they make me feel _____.

I believe, God, that you made me. You want me to be _____
and give you praise by _____.

Thank you for other people in my life, especially _____.

Lord, I love you and I want to praise you always. Amen.

Celebrate God's Creation

A page for you to color

God loved Adam and Eve very much and wanted them to be happy. God gave them everything they needed including all kinds of good food to eat. But God warned them not to eat the fruit from the tree in the middle of the garden.

Adam and Eve were tempted and they disobeyed God. As soon as they ate the forbidden fruit, they realized that they had done a bad thing. They were sad that they had disobeyed God, and they even tried to hide from God, but no one can ever hide from God. Do you know why? Look at the clues in the graph below to find the answer.

As an example, to find what 1△ would be, follow row 1 across with your left finger. Now follow the triangle row up and down with your right finger. At what letter does the number 1 and the triangle meet? The letter "R" is your answer for 1△.

Adam and Eve
Genesis 3:1–13

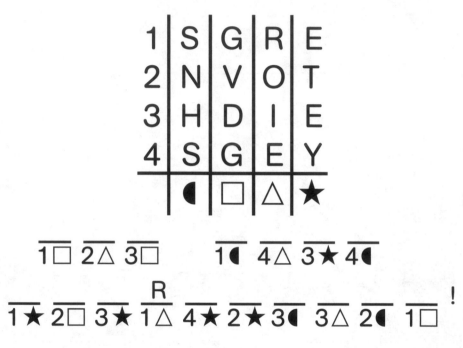

When you are finished with the puzzle, color the picture.

A Promised Savior
Genesis 3:20–24

When Adam and Eve disobeyed God, they sinned. This first sin is called "Original Sin."

God punished them by making them leave the beautiful garden. He told them that for the rest of their lives they would have to suffer and work hard. Yet God did not just leave them in their misery, but offered hope to them. God said that some day a messiah would come and save the world from its sin.

What you need:
• access to a photocopier
• scissors
• glue
• crayons

What you do:
Photocopy puzzle A and puzzle B. Then cut out the puzzle A pieces. Match the numbered pieces of the puzzle A to the numbered squares of puzzle B. The first group of squares are filled in with parts of a picture. They contain a mystery picture. Use your crayons to add color to the finished picture.

Puzzle A.

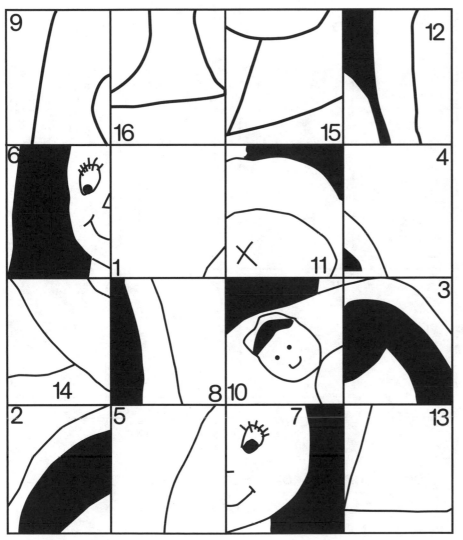

God kept this promise! After Adam and Eve lived, many, many years passed before the Messiah (or Savior) came. Do you know who that was? Jesus was the promised Savior!

Puzzle B.

1	2	3	4
5	6	7	8
9	10	11	12
13	14	15	16

…but when the completion of the time came, God sent his Son, born of a woman. (Gal 4:4)

Cain and Abel

Genesis 4:1-16

Adam and Eve had a baby boy whom they named Cain. Time passed and Cain got a new brother, Abel. When the two boys grew up, Cain became a farmer. He tilled the soil and grew vegetables and fruits. Abel became a shepherd and took care of the sheep.

One day both of the brothers wanted to offer God a gift. So Cain brought something from his garden, and Abel brought the first born lamb from his flock.

God liked Abel's offering the best. Cain knew this and became angry and jealous. God said to Cain, "Why are you so angry? If you did good, then hold your head high!" But Cain didn't listen. He was so jealous that he killed his brother. Cain knew he did a bad thing. God punished him for acting out his jealous feelings.

The Green Monster

Sometimes when someone has something that we really want, we might experience a bad feeling inside. This is jealousy. Sometimes people call jealousy the "Green Monster." It can make us want to say and do hurtful things to others.

As children of our loving God, we don't say or do those mean things. We take control of our actions.

cut - - - → ← - - - cut

fold → ← fold

**Plan of attack
if the green monster comes:**

1. **Pray to God for help.**

2. **Think of something nice about the person of whom you are jealous.**

3. **Give that person a compliment.**

4. **Pray for the person of whom you are jealous**

cut - - - → ← - - - cut

Cut along the lines. Fold it in half. Glue or tape the two halves together. Now look at the picture. What do you see? Turn it upside down. Which of the two would you rather be? If the green monster ever comes, find this card, read it, and carry out the "plan of attack" on the back.

Many years after Adam and Eve lived on the earth, God made Noah. Noah pleased God because he tried very hard to be good.

At the time, there were many people on earth who lived in sin, and God was angry with them. So God decided to punish them by flooding the earth.

Since Noah was a good man, God wanted to save him and his family from the flood. God told Noah to build a big boat called an *ark*. Then God told Noah to take two of every kind of animal onto the ark. When the big boat was finished, Noah and his family went inside it and closed the door. God let it rain for forty days and forty nights. The earth was flooded and everything was destroyed except the people and animals in the ark.

Afterwards, God promised Noah that he would never send another flood to destroy the earth. He made a covenant, that is, an agreement, with Noah.

```
M Q S G N H W B
E N O P I G N I
A T U V H T C V
R T S T S I L I
J H I H E G L L
Q Y T A H N X A
A Z C E T O N D
E V O H T F A G
N T I V E L F U
A N H A E E S Y
P J A T S E T M
S R B S H B W N
Y K L I E D E E
```

24

Noah
Genesis 6,7,9:8–17

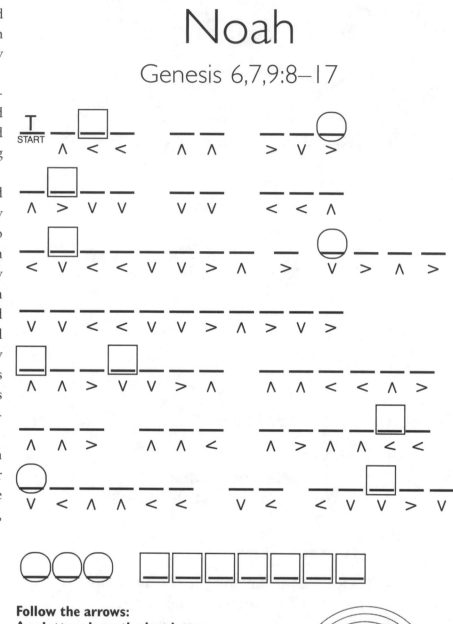

Follow the arrows:
^ = letter above the last letter
v = letter below the last letter
< = letter to the left of last letter
> = letter to the right of last letter

Figure out what God said to Noah. Starting at the bold letter "T" near the middle of the letter chart, follow in the direction of the arrowheads to the next letter; write that letter on the line.

Some of the letters above are inside a circle. Unscramble them and put them in the circles below. Other letters are inside a square. Unscramble them and put them in the squares below. The answer will tell you the sign of God's covenant with Noah.

After the Rain
Genesis 8:6–14

After the rain stopped, Noah opened one of the windows of the ark and let a dove out to fly around the earth. Since there was no dry spot to land, the dove came back. A week went by and Noah let the dove go out again. The dove came back with an olive branch in its mouth. That meant the water level went down and some of the treetops were showing. Seven days later he sent the dove out again. It never returned. Noah knew, then, that the bird found a place to live. The earth was drying out.

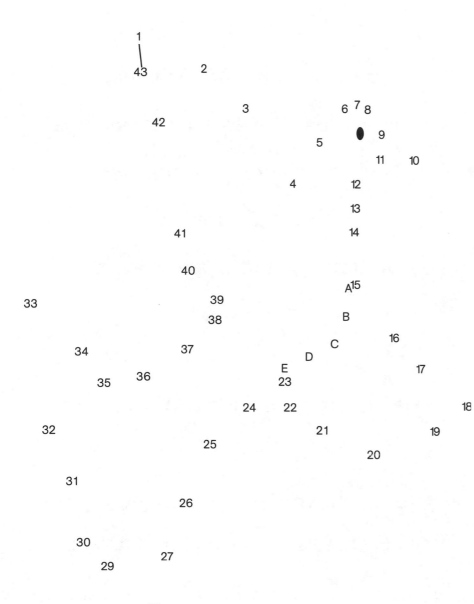

Connect the numbers, then connect the letters.
Draw an olive branch where it should go:

The dove carrying the olive branch is a symbol of peace.

When we hear and retell stories about our parents and grandparents, we feel a connection to our personal heritage. Even if they have died, we feel we are keeping them alive by sharing what we know. In the same way, hearing accounts of the Old Testament patriarchs give the children a sense of belonging to an important family, namely, God's family. As you talk about the biblical stories this month, it would be well to point out the human emotions that come into play: Sarah's doubt, Abraham's grief and fear, Esau's fickleness, the jealousy of Jacob's sons. You will see that the patriarchs were normal, touchable people just like us.

November Prayer

O God,

From the time I was a baby,

you have watched over me.

Thank you for your love and your care.

I am grateful for all your gifts,

especially for…

(say out loud or in silence some things

you are thankful for).

From ages past your people

have known your love and goodness.

With them I pray:

O give thanks to the Lord, for he is good,

for his steadfast love endures forever.

(Ps 136:1)

God Calls Abram
Genesis 12:1–5; 15:1–6; 17:1–9

After Noah died and many, many years passed, God spoke to a man named Abram. God asked Abram to leave the town of Ur, where he was living, and go to another place. That was not an easy thing for Abram to do, but he believed in God and knew that God must be obeyed, so he did as he was asked. God saw how faithful Abram was. God blessed him, saying, "Look up at the sky and count the stars if you can. Just so will your descendants be."

Abram trusted that God would be true to his promise. When Abram was ninety-nine years old, God made a covenant with him and changed his name to Abraham, which means "father of a multitude."

When you were born, your parents gave you a name. It is a very special name. Did you know that God knew what your name would be even before your parents did?

What you need:
- paper
- pencils
- crayons or markers

Find thirteen six-pointed stars in this picture and color them in.

Collects **R**ace Cars

H**O**nest

Has a **B**ig Heart

Eats Pizza

Likes to **R**ide his Bike

Smar**T**

I have called you by name. You are mine.
Isaiah 43:1

Make a sign with your name on it, like the sample here. Write some things about yourself using the letters of your name. On the bottom of the sign, put the quote from Isaiah 43:1.

27

Abraham was married to Sarah. The couple loved each other very much, but Sarah had not been able to bear children. Now they were quite old. One hot day, when Abraham was sitting outside his tent, he looked up and saw three men standing close by. Abraham jumped to greet them. He said, "Come and have lunch with us," then he and Sarah prepared a wonderful meal for their guests. Later on, when Sarah was inside the tent, they told Abraham, "Next year your wife, Sarah, will have a baby boy."

From inside, Sarah had heard them talking. She knew she was too old to have children and so she laughed at what they said. At first, Abraham thought his three visitors were men. But then he realized his guests were God and two angels! God said, "Why did Sarah laugh?" Then God told Abraham something important for everyone to remember. To figure out the cryptoquip, look at the letter under the line, for example "Y", and see that it refers to an "N" and write that letter on the line.

Abraham and Sarah
Genesis 18:1–15

A = G	E = D	K = B	Q = H	W = O
B = M	F = L	M = I	R = W	Y = N
C = P	J = S	P = T	T = E	

Y W P Q M Y A   M J

M B C W J J M K F T

R M P Q   A W E

Isaac
Genesis 22:1–19

Find and circle the ram in the bushes.

Just as the Lord had said, Sarah had a baby boy. His parents named him Isaac. Abraham and Sarah loved Isaac very much!

God decided to test Abraham. When Isaac was a young boy, God said, "Take Isaac and slay him and make him a sacrifice to me." Those were hard words for Abraham to hear! He was very, very sad about what God wanted him to do. But still, Abraham believed God would make things turn out all right in the end. And so he took Isaac up to the mountain. He told his son, "We will go and make a sacrifice to the Lord." Isaac said to his dad, "But where is the lamb for the sacrifice?" Abraham said, "God will provide a lamb."

When they got to the top of the mountain, Abraham tied up Isaac and was about to slay him when an angel appeared and stopped him. "Do not lay a hand on him. God has seen your faith!" Abraham looked around. He saw a ram in the bushes. He took the creature and offered it to God, who blessed Abraham for his great faith.

God had never intended for Abraham to kill Isaac. He just wanted to test him. But now, think a minute: In the New Testament, there is a father who gave up his son. Do you know who that father is?

JESUS

"Behold the lamb of God..." (Jn1:29)

Hold this sign up to a mirror. What is the son's name?

When Isaac grew up, he married a woman named Rebekah and together they had twin boys. The first to be born was Esau. Do you know why they named him that? "Esau" means "hairy," and the baby was very hairy! The second twin was named Jacob. In those days, the firstborn held a special place of honor in the family. He received more than all the rest of the children when the dad died. This was called the birthright.

One day, many years later, Jacob was in the tent, cooking a delicious stew. Esau came in from hunting. Esau said to his brother, "Give me some of your stew!" Jacob said, "I will give you some stew if you give me your birthright." At that moment, Esau only cared about his growling stomach. And so, for a bowl of stew, he gave Jacob his birthright.

As the years passed, Isaac grew old and blind. It was time to give Esau his special blessing. So when Esau was out hunting, Jacob dressed in his brother's clothes and put lamb skins on his arms to make them feel hairy. Then he went to visit his dad. Isaac thought he was Esau, and Jacob received a firstborn son's blessing.

Jacob
Genesis 25:24–34, 27:1–40

Esau and Jacob

Take a pencil and make Jacob look like Esau

Circle all the things Jacob may have put in his stew.

grass · ball · salt · socks · glue · corn · potatoes · bugs · orange · leaves · carrots · peas · celery · Jacob's Stew · meat · cake · ice cream cone · tomatoes · onions · candy

30

Jacob's Sons
Genesis 30:21; 35:23–26; Joshua 14–19:51

Jacob had twelve sons. He also had a daughter named Dinah. It's important to know the names of Jacob's sons because a long time after Jacob died, the kingdom of Israel was divided into twelve sections and each territory was named after one of Jacob's sons. When you read Scripture, you will come across these names. For example, during Advent, you might hear this Scripture passage from Matthew 4:15–16:

"Land of Zebulun, land of Naphtali…the people who sat in darkness have seen a great light…."

In the Name Search below, find the names of Jacob's sons. The letters of each name can be found above, below, or next to each other. Look for them any way except diagonally. You can use the same letter more than once. The first name is done for you.

Reuben
Judah
Gad
Zebulun
Simeon
Dan
Asher
Joseph
Levi
Naphtali
Issachar
Benjamin

```
K  L  U  N  P  A  C  B
B  U  D  A  H  S  H  E
E  J  M  I  S  S  A  N
Z  N  E  B  R  I  R  J
F  A  O  U  E  V  G  A
H  P  N  A  L  D  A  M
T  I  H  S  O  J  N  I
A  L  E  R  S  E  P  H
```

Can you name an important town that was located in the land of Judah? Take your Bible and look up Matthew 2:6.

Write the name of the town: _____

Who was born there? If you are not sure, read Matthew 2:1.

_____

Jacob loved all his sons, but he favored his eleventh son, Joseph. One day Jacob gave Joseph a gift. It was a beautiful colorful coat. That made his older brothers jealous!

Then something else got them more irritated. Joseph told them about the dreams he had been having and what they meant. In these dreams, Joseph was put above his brothers. This made them very upset and they did things they later regretted. They threw Joseph into a pit, then sold him as a slave to some people going to Egypt. The brothers took Joseph's colorful coat and brought it to their dad, saying, "Joseph was killed by a wild animal!"

Joseph's Colorful Coat
Genesis 37:2–36

Look at Joseph's coats.
Circle the coat that does not match the rest.

Now go to the booklet on the next page. Cut this page out, or make a copy of it. Color the pictures, then fold the booklet on the dotted lines so that page one is in front.

Joseph's Colorful Coat

Jacob gave his son the neatest coat
you've ever seen!
It was purple, orange, red, and blue,
yellow, brown, and green.

1.

Joseph wore it with a smile;
He was grateful and very glad.
He told his dad, "I love this coat!
It's the best I've ever had."

2.

Joseph's brothers saw the gift.
"Where's ours?" they wondered then.
"We should get the same as him,"
Said those jealous, angry men.

3.

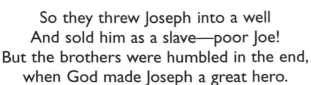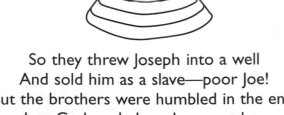

So they threw Joseph into a well
And sold him as a slave—poor Joe!
But the brothers were humbled in the end,
when God made Joseph a great hero.

4.

Away from home, Joseph was very sad and lonely. He missed his dad and suffered many things, but he never forgot about God. He prayed that God would help him, and God did! God gave Joseph the gift of figuring out the meaning of dreams.

Years later the Pharaoh, who was the king of Egypt, heard about Joseph. The Pharaoh had a couple of scary dreams. One was about seven fat cows and seven skinny cows. He called on Joseph to interpret his dreams. Joseph told him that the fat cows meant there would be enough food in the land for seven years. The skinny cows meant that there would be seven years of famine, that is, a time when no food would grow. Pharaoh listened to what Joseph said, and made sure that enough food would be stored up for the years of famine ahead. Joseph became a big hero!

Some days, things just don't go the way we want them to go. We get mad or frustrated, or we have to do something we can't stand doing! If something really bothers you, be sure to talk about it with someone you trust and who can help you. Then, like Joseph, offer up the hard things to God. Pray and always remember that God is with you.

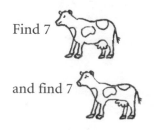

Find 7

and find 7

Joseph in Egypt
Genesis 37:12—36; 38—41:57

December Prayer

Jesus,

During this time of Advent,

I am thinking about how you

came to earth

to fulfill the Father's plan.

You are the promised Messiah,

the One for whom

the world waited so long!

Stay in my heart

where I will adore you and thank you

forever and ever. Amen.

To Parents and Catechists:

The Bible stories covered in this month's activity pages carry a strong message: God is indeed with his people. In the Advent and Christmas liturgies we hear the same wonderful news: Maranatha—"Our Lord has come," and Emmanuel—"God is with us." In the first activity, about baby Moses, the children hear that God is a very personal God, who doesn't just remain "out there" but who cared about us even before we were born. God helped the Israelite slaves escape from the bullies of Egypt and proved time after time that he was with his people even until the coming of Jesus, Emmanuel.

Remember Pharaoh, the king of Egypt, from the story about Joseph on page 34? Long after Joseph lived, another Pharaoh ruled Egypt. But this new king did not remember how Joseph had helped Egypt, and he made the Israelites who lived there his slaves. In fact, Pharaoh was scared that the Israelites would become more powerful than Egypt, and so he did a very bad thing. He ordered all the Israelite baby boys to be killed!

One Israelite mother just had a new baby boy whom she loved so much. For three months she hid him from the Egyptian soldiers, but she knew she couldn't hide him forever. So she made a basket and put her baby boy in it. Then she hid it among the reeds by the river. When she came down to the river to bathe, Pharaoh's daughter found the baby and kept him. She named him Moses.

Baby Moses
Exodus 1:22—2:10

Circle the things the Israelite mother put in the basket with the baby to keep him safe and happy.

God made you and he thinks you are very special. There is a message from the Bible hidden in baby Moses' basket. Write down the first letter, B, and every other letter after that.

— — — — —　—　— — — — —

— — —　— — —　— — — —

— —　— — — —　— — —

Jeremiah 1:4–5

36

Moses is Called

Exodus 2:11–25; 3:15

Find the list of words in the word search. Then, using these words in the order given, see if you can retell the story of Moses and the burning bush.

```
G D R E H P E H S
O F H T S G O E P
D R S E S A M B N
S E U L R D L R A
E E B A A I K E I
S O H F Z V F W D
O P T P Y G E S I
M C A N A A N S M
```

Moses   Bush
Pharaoh   Fire
Hebrews   God
Slaves   Egypt
Midian   Free
Shepherd   Canaan

Even though Moses grew up in the king's court, he loved his own people, the Israelites (also know as "Hebrews"). He felt bad that they were slaves and were forced to do so much work. Once Moses tried to defend the Israelites, but Pharaoh found out and became very angry with Moses. Out of fear, Moses ran away to a place called Midian, where he lived as a shepherd.

One day when Moses was out with the sheep, he noticed a fascinating thing. It was a bush on fire; yet the fire kept on blazing without harming the bush! Moses went closer to look at it. Then, from the burning bush he heard God's voice.

God told Moses that he had heard Israel's cry for help and that Moses should return to Egypt. Through Moses, God would free the Israelites and bring them to the land of Canaan.

Moses told his brother Aaron about the burning bush. Then, together, Moses and Aaron relayed God's message to the elders of the Israelites. They told them that God saw the misery of the people of Israel and would lead them out of slavery in Egypt into a land flowing with milk and honey. The people believed Moses and Aaron, and bowed in worship to God.

Moses and Aaron then went to the Pharaoh and told them that the God of Israel had something to say. Use the code of numbers and letters to find out God's message.

But Pharaoh didn't believe in the God of Israel. He wouldn't do what Moses asked. God said to Moses, "Tell Aaron to throw down his staff in front of Pharaoh." When Aaron did this, the staff turned into something amazing. But did it scare Pharaoh? No. He was still stubborn.

Pharaoh is Stubborn
Exodus 4:27–31; 5:1; 7:8–13

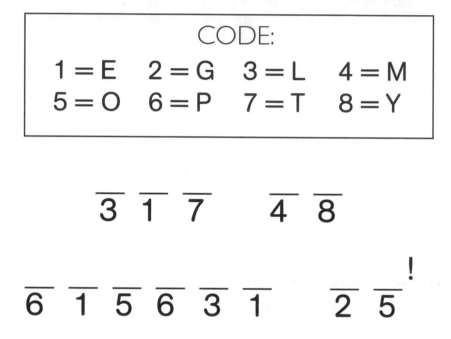

CODE:

1 = E	2 = G	3 = L	4 = M
5 = O	6 = P	7 = T	8 = Y

$$\overline{3}\ \overline{1}\ \overline{7}\quad \overline{4}\ \overline{8}$$

$$\overline{6}\ \overline{1}\ \overline{5}\ \overline{6}\ \overline{3}\ \overline{1}\quad \overline{2}\ \overline{5}\,!$$

What did Aaron's staff turn into?
Connect the dots to find out.

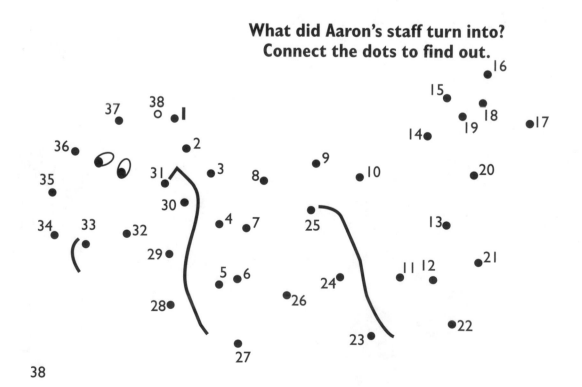

The Ten Plagues
Exodus 7:14—11:10

Now if you could tell Pharaoh one thing, what would you say? Here's a hint: look at the list of plagues. The underlined letters, in order, from top to bottom, spell out what you might tell the king of Egypt. Write this sentence on the lines below.

1. Ugh! Water is turned into blood!

2. Yikes! Freaky frogs are everywhere!

3. Get out the calamine lotion! Here come the gnats!

4. Surprise! Hear and see all the flies!

5. It's no jest—pesky pestilence! (The livestock was killed and Pharaoh grows tense.)

6. Troubles and toils! Our skin is full of boils!

7. The land was nailed with hail and more hail! (At the sight of destruction, Pharaoh paled.)

8. Are all eyes focussed? Yes, it's locusts! The grasshoppers are eating everything!

9. It's very scary! Three days of darkness feels so eerie.

10. It's bad; it's sad—the firstborn of every Egyptian and animal are dead!

Since Pharaoh would not listen to Moses, God sent ten plagues, which are really bad things, to the Egyptians. God sent the plagues one at a time. When Pharaoh did not let the Israelites go after the first plague, God sent the next plague, and so on through all ten.

Pretend you are an Egyptian television reporter at the time of the plagues (imagine that they had TV in those times). Tell your viewers about what is happening in Egypt, and start by using the sentences on the left. Then describe everyone's reaction to the plagues, including your personal feelings about what is happening in Egypt right now. You can look up the story in the Bible using the citation above for more information about these plagues.

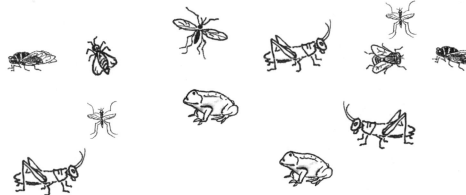

"Pharaoh, would you please just…

____ ____ ____ ____ ____ ____ ____ ____ !"

39

Before God sent the tenth plague, he told Moses that each Israelite family must find a perfect lamb and kill it. Then they were to take some of the animal's blood and put it on the outside of their door. That way, no first-born Israelite child would die, because when the angel of the Lord saw the blood on the door, he would *pass over* that house. That is why the Hebrew people came to have a celebration called "Passover."

In the New Testament, we think of Jesus being like the Passover lamb who died to save each of us. Because of him, we can go to heaven. John the Baptist said about Jesus: "Here is the Lamb of God who takes away the sin of the world!" (John 1:29).

God told the Israelites that they could roast the lamb and celebrate a feast. After that, however, they had to be ready to leave Egypt immediately. Then God sent the tenth plague. When Pharaoh found his firstborn son dead, he told Moses to take all the Israelites and leave Egypt.

The First Passover
Exodus 12:1–34

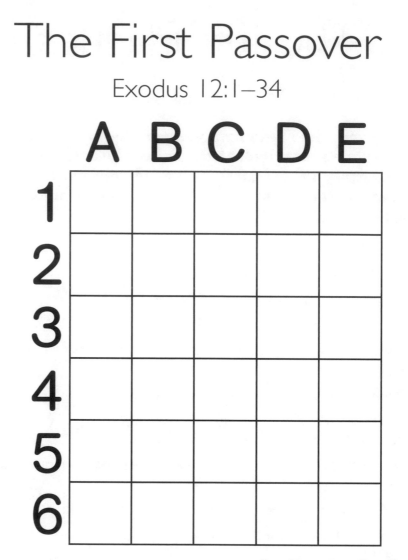

Here is a symbol of Jesus, the paschal (Passover) lamb. Copy the smaller squares onto the corresponding squares above.

Find the Pharaoh that matches the first one.

40

Parting of the Red Sea

Exodus 14:15–31

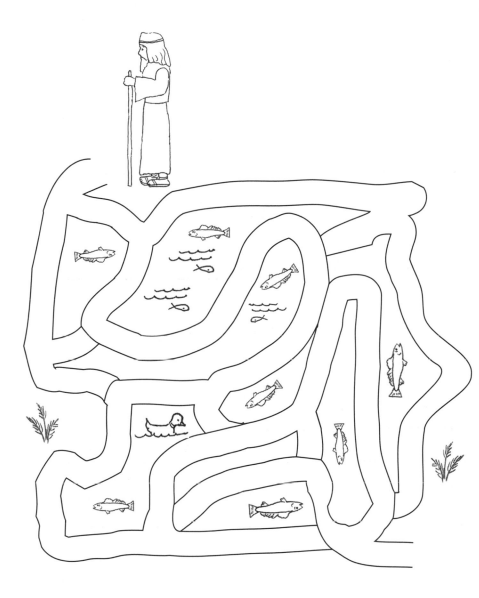

After that first Passover, Moses led the Israelites out of Egypt. Six hundred thousand men left with their wives and children and animals. God led them by a pillar of cloud during the day and a pillar of fire at night. After they were gone, Pharaoh was sorry he let the Israelites leave Egypt. He wanted his slaves back! So Pharaoh sent his army after them.

By that time, Moses and the people were at the Red Sea, but they didn't have boats to get them across. They had nowhere to go and Pharaoh's army was close behind!

Moses had great faith in God. He lifted his shepherd's staff over the water. All of a sudden, the sea split in two, making a path of dry land for the Israelites to walk across. As they walked across the path, the water stayed up like a wall on both sides of them. Once they were safely across the sea, Moses stretched out his staff again and the walls of water tumbled back into the sea. And guess what happened to the Egyptian army? They were all swept into the sea and drowned.

Help Moses and the Israelites walk through the Red Sea.

The Jewish people refer to the first five books of the Bible as the "Torah." We use another term when we talk about this group of books. We call it the "Pentateuch."

Look at the contents page in your Bible. Find the books that make up the Pentateuch (sounds like pen-ta-took) and write them down.

The Pentateuch

See how many words you can make using the following letters:

P e n t a t e u c h

Can you find at least 20 three-lettered words?	Can you find at least 20 four-lettered words?	Can you find at least 15 five-lettered words?
cat	tent	peach

January Prayer

Dear Lord,

Every day I hear your voice

speaking to me

through different things that happen.

You call me to help out

where help is needed.

You call me to share

where someone is lacking.

You call me to be patient

where things are mixed-up

and not the way I want them to be.

Help me not only to hear your voice,

but to listen, and then do

what is pleasing to you.

Amen.

To Parents and Catechists:

January is a time when we like to make some new resolutions. This month's activity pages give subtle suggestions for this, such as memorizing the Ten Commandments, always respecting God's name, or helping out with the chores as in "Children of the Desert." The craft for the Ark of the Covenant suggests actions of good will, while the activity about the complaining Israelites points out that nobody, not even God, likes a grumbler.

After leaving Egypt, Moses and the people of Israel traveled for three months. When they came to Mount Sinai, they set up camp.

Moses told the people that God would be revealed to them. So they bathed themselves and got ready for that special day. When the time came, they heard thunder and saw lightning and a thick cloud. They stood at the base of the mountain. God came down on them in fire and smoke, and the mountain shook. The people were not allowed to climb the mountain because it was sacred, which is another word for holy.

Moses went up and spoke with God, and God gave him the law that the people were to follow. These laws are called the Ten Commandments.

Now, take the answer letter at the end of each line, and match it to the numbers below (one problem has been done for you).

The Ten Commandments
Exodus 19:1–25; 20:1–21

**What is another name for the Ten Commandments?
Figure it out by solving the math problems.**

$\Box + 4 = 10$ …Answer = A

$8 + \Box = 10$ …Answer = C

$7 + \Box = 10$ …Answer = D

$\boxed{1} + 9 = 10$ …Answer = U

$6 + \Box = 10$ …Answer = L

$\Box + 3 = 10$ …Answer = E

$\Box + 5 = 10$ …Answer = O

$2 + \Box = 10$ …Answer = G

Another name for the Ten Commandments is

"The $\underline{\quad}\ \underline{\quad}\ \underline{\quad}\ \underline{\quad}\ \underline{\quad}\ \underline{\quad}\ \underline{\quad}\ \underline{U}\ \underline{\quad}$ "
           3 7 2 6 4 5 8 1 7

God's Law Is for Everyone

Exodus 20:1–17; Deuteronomy 5:1–21

1	You shall not have strange gods before me	6	You shall not commit adultery
2	You shall not take the name of the Lord your God in vain	7	You shall not steal
3	Remember to keep holy the Lord's day	8	You shall not bear false witness against your neighbor
4	Honor your father and mother	9	You shall not covet your neighbor's wife
5	You shall not kill	10	You shall not covet your neighbor's goods

God wanted the Israelites to know exactly what they should do and what they should not do, and this is why he gave Moses the Ten Commandments. In fact, these laws were so important that they were inscribed on stone tablets and later placed in a very important place, called the Ark of the Covenant.

God wrote these laws not only for the Israelites but for everyone throughout the ages. When God made you, he put these commandments in your heart to help guide you in life. Scripture tells us, "I will put my law within them, and I will write it on their hearts…" (Jeremiah 31:33).

Here are some flash cards you can use to help you remember the Ten Commandments. Cut them out (or make a copy to cut out) and put the number of each commandment on the back of the flash card. See if you can memorize the Commandments, then quiz yourself.

"I am the Lord, your God…"

Names of God

When you speak to people of importance, you show respect by how you address them. Sometimes you don't even say their real names. You call a king, "Your Highness," a judge, "Your Honor," and a bishop, "Your Excellency." Now, if God is more mighty than all the important people on earth, shouldn't everyone speak God's name with reverence and awe? The second commandment tells us to do so. In Old Testament times, the people felt God was so holy that they didn't even pronounce their name for God.

In Exodus 3:14, God tells Moses what to say to the Israelites when they ask who sent Moses to them. Use the pictograph to figure out what this name is.

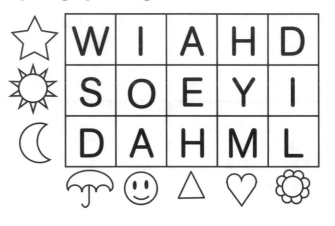

As an act of love toward your Creator, make a promise to always use God's name with reverence. Color the sign on the next page; hang it in your home for everyone to see.

The Israelites also addressed God with this name:

I WILL PRAISE YOUR NAME FOREVER

God showed the people of Israel that he was with them in the desert in many different ways. When the Israelites were hungry, God sent quail so they could have meat. God also sent a special kind of food that was like bread. Every morning the people went out and collected this food as it lay like frost on the ground. It fed them for years.

What did the Israelites call this food? To find out, write the word for the picture on the lines. The squares going down will spell out the name for the "bread" from heaven.

When the Israelites were thirsty, God told Moses to hit the rock at Horeb with his staff. When Moses did, something flowed out that quenched the peoples' thirst. What was it? Do the same as you did for the puzzle above to find out the answer.

Food from Heaven
Exodus 16:1–36; 17:1–7

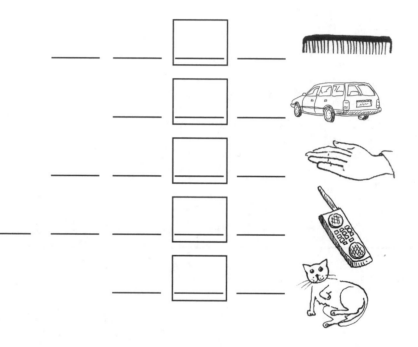

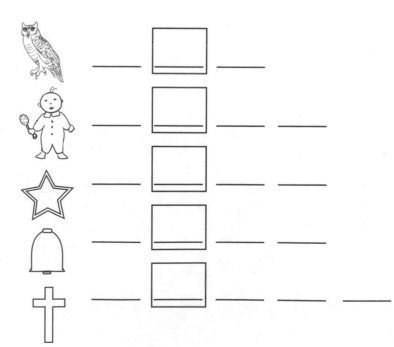

48

Children in the Desert

Oh children of the Israelites, you boys and girls like me,
You must have been so happy when the Pharaoh set you free!

You crossed the sea with Moses and camped with your Moms and Dads,
just knowing God was with you made you feel so safe and glad.

As all children through the ages, you sang and laughed and played;
you ate, you slept, obeyed your folks and, of course, you prayed.

But one thing I've always wondered—did you have some work to do?
Oh, children in the desert, what were some of the chores for you?

Here are some imaginary Israelite children, living in the desert. They each have chores to do!

While they were on their way to accomplish their tasks, they spotted items, bugs, or animals on the road. Follow the path of the objects each of them saw in order to figure out what chore they had to do.

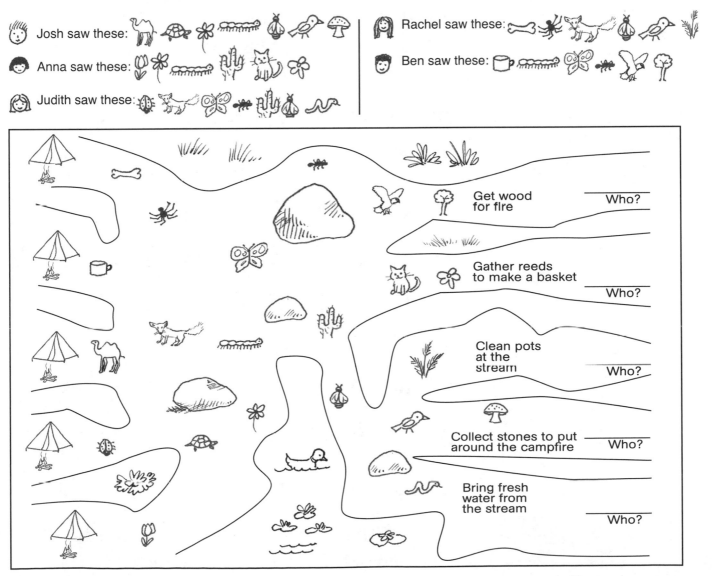

During our stay on earth, God wants to be known with the eyes of faith. God wants us to understand that he is with us and loves us, even if we cannot see God. In order for us to know how much God cares for us, he made covenants with his people throughout the centuries. A covenant is an important agreement between two people or two groups. Both promise to keep their part of the bargain.

Oftentimes, God's people sinned and were not faithful to the covenant. But God is always faithful!

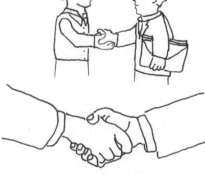

What Is a Covenant?

Word Search
In this word search, find these words which are synonyms for the word "covenant."

Deal	Vow	Covenant
Pact	Bound	Agreement
Treaty	Word of honor	Contract
Bond	Oath	Pledge
Bargain	Obligation	Commitment

```
B O U N D E G D E L P
A T C A P M L Q C B V
R C S Y T A E R T H O
G A G R E E M E N T W
A R U D B O N D V A L
I T N E M T I M M O C
N N O I T A G I L B O
W O R D O F H O N O R
Z C O V E N A N T Q P
```

The Lord is faithful in all his words and holy in all his works. (Psalm 145:13)

The Ark of the Covenant

Exodus 35–40

God told Moses and the people to build a meeting tent that they could carry with them as they traveled. It would be God's special dwelling place. Their best carpenters built it with the finest wood, and decorated it with gold, jewels, and beautiful cloths which were given by the people. There was a place for people to make offerings to God and to burn sweet-smelling incense.

A marvelous golden box was made with two angels on it. This was the "ark" where the Ten Commandments, inscribed on stone tablets, were kept. Later, Moses put a special curtain up to keep the ark separate from the rest of the meeting tent. When all the work was done, God was very pleased.

Here is a picture of the Ark of the Covenant. What was kept inside?

God, I will try to do something nice for someone. I will _____ _____ _____	God, thank you for the things you give me, especially _____ _____ _____
God, I love you and someday I want to be _____ _____ _____	O God, stay close to me and please help _____ _____ _____

God wants to make a dwelling place for him in your heart.

Color and decorate the heart on this page. Cut it out and trace it on a piece of red construction paper. Now, cut that heart out. Staple the two hearts together only at the lines. (Leave the top of the heart open like a pocket.)

Cut out the boxes containing sentences on the previous page and put them in your "heart."

The Israelites Grumble

Numbers 13–14

Find the twelve Israelite spies who are observing the Canaanites. Here is a sample of one of the Israelites.

After a year at their camp by Mount Sinai, Moses sent twelve men to Canaan to see what the people and the land were like. God had promised to bring the Israelites to a place flowing with milk and honey, and Canaan was just that.

But the men whom Moses sent came back frightened, and they grumbled about the Canaanites. "They are too big and too strong for us. We will never be able to conquer the land!" The Israelites heard this and began to wail, saying, "Why didn't we just stay in Egypt?"

God was angry with the Israelites' whining. After all God had done for them, they were still stubborn and unbelieving! God told them that they would wander in the desert as punishment for their lack of faith. God told them that only their children would enter Canaan one day, and prosper in that land flowing with milk and honey. God remained true to his promise.

To find out how many years the Israelites wandered in the desert, take a black marker or crayon and cross out the first letter, "B," and every other letter after that.

BFTOSRKTMY JYCEZAQRNS

To Parents and Catechists:

This month's activities focus on people in the Bible who were great not just because of what they did but because of the virtues that were so much a part of their lives. Around Valentine's Day, stress the idea that it's not so much what you do that's important; what matters is the love that motivates one's actions. Look at Joshua, Gideon, Deborah, Samson, and Ruth: because of their love and intention to serve the Lord, they succeeded in their tasks, despite all obstacles. The pop-up sign is a fun craft that reminds the children of God's presence. "Make an Israelite" challenges them to recall the Bible stories covered in the first part of the school year.

February Prayer

O God,
Please help me to start today
with a happy attitude.

Help me to remember
that no matter what may go wrong
you are there to help me through it.

When things go just the way I want
then help me to remember
to include you in my celebration.

With all my heart, I love you.
Amen.

The Walls of Jericho

Joshua 6:1–20

In the wall below, find the bricks that have a dot in them. What letter is in that brick? In order, from left to right and top to bottom, write each of those letters down. Then, when you feel alone or afraid, remember these words which God said to Joshua (1:5):

Finally, it was time for the Israelites to enter the promised land!

Jericho was a big city in the land of Canaan. It had a giant wall around it. God told Joshua to take his warriors and march around the city of Jericho once a day for six days. Then, on the seventh day, God told them to march around the city seven times. As the priests blew their trumpets and the people shouted, the walls around Jericho came tumbling down.

The Israelites surely were afraid to fight the Canaanites. But they knew that if God was on their side, they would win. And they did! As they conquered the land of Canaan, Joshua divided it among the twelve tribes of Israel (remember our lesson from page 31, about the names of the twelve tribes?).

— —————— ——————

— — —   ———— — ———;

— — ——————   ———————

            . Joshua 1:5

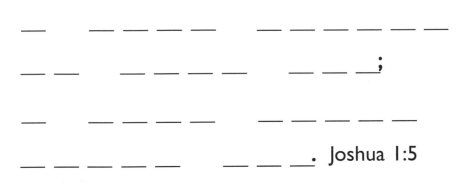

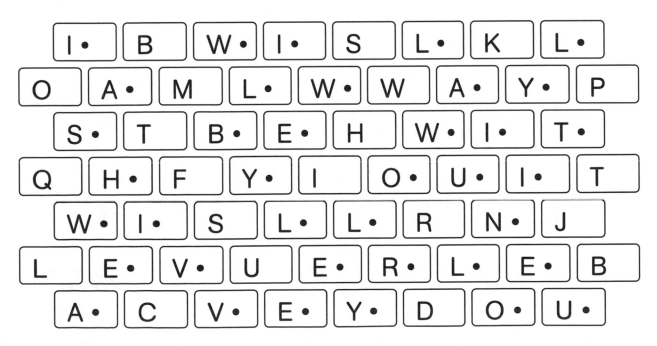

My strength and my courage is the Lord and he has been my savior.
(Psalm 118:14)

Before Joshua died he told the people, "You must serve the one, true God!" He reminded them of their history, of the faith of Abraham, Isaac, Jacob, and Moses. He told them to remember the marvelous deeds the Lord worked when the Israelites were slaves in Egypt and when they crossed the Red Sea and overcame Pharaoh's army. "Fear the Lord and be his faithful servants!" he said.

Then Joshua said something that many people still remember today. Read the clues. Write the answers at the right of each clue, every letter over one number. Then, place each letter over the same number in the mystery message below. Figure out Joshua's famous saying.

Joshua
Joshua 24

CLUES

1. The opposite of cold. $\overline{18}\ \overline{14}\ \overline{33}$

2. Many people eat three of these a day. $\overline{6}\ \overline{23}\ \overline{1}\ \overline{27}\ \overline{16}$

3. Female chickens that lay eggs. $\overline{13}\ \overline{35}\ \overline{9}\ \overline{28}$

4. A locked box where you can put money. $\overline{2}\ \overline{8}\ \overline{3}\ \overline{32}$

5. The back part of your foot. $\overline{34}\ \overline{29}\ \overline{17}\ \overline{20}$

6. The opposite of high. $\overline{36}\ \overline{19}\ \overline{24}$

7. You do this with a car. $\overline{10}\ \overline{38}\ \overline{25}\ \overline{31}\ \overline{7}$

8. A musical instrument you hit with sticks. $\overline{39}\ \overline{5}\ \overline{15}\ \overline{11}$

9. The opposite of wet. $\overline{21}\ \overline{30}\ \overline{12}$

10. The hair on a lamb is called this. $\overline{22}\ \overline{37}\ \overline{4}\ \overline{26}$

$\overline{1}\ \overline{2}\quad \overline{3}\ \overline{4}\ \overline{5}\quad \overline{6}\ \overline{7}\quad \overline{8}\ \overline{9}\ \overline{10}\quad \overline{11}\ \overline{12}$

$\overline{13}\ \overline{14}\ \overline{15}\ \overline{16}\ \overline{17}\ \overline{18}\ \overline{19}\ \overline{20}\ \overline{21}\quad \overline{22}\ \overline{23}\quad \overline{24}\ \overline{25}\ \overline{26}\ \overline{27}$

$\overline{28}\ \overline{29}\ \overline{30}\ \overline{31}\ \overline{32}\quad \overline{33}\ \overline{34}\ \overline{35}\quad \overline{36}\ \overline{37}\ \overline{38}\ \overline{39}.$ Joshua 24:15

Gideon

Judges 6:36–40; 7:1–25

It was important to Gideon to know God was with him. Here is a pop-up sign you can make to help you remember that God is with you:

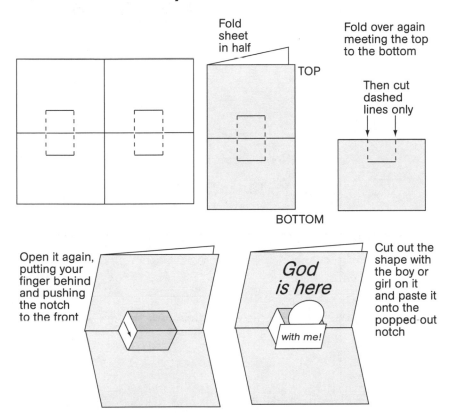

What you need:

Crayons, scissors, glue, and access to a photocopy machine.

1. **First photocopy the girl or boy shape to the right at 200% and cut it out. Then photocopy the "God is here" page.**
2. **Color the "God is here" page. Hold the sheet horizontally and fold the sheet in half vertically with the words "God is here" facing front. Glue the two halves together. Then fold it in half again from top to bottom.**
3. **Cut the two slits through the back fold, as shown. Open the "card" and pull the cut strip through. Bend it in the center so it stands up.**
4. **Cut out and color the "with me!" sign out (girl for girls, or boy for boys). Glue it to the bottom standing strip.**
5. **Place it on your dresser or nightstand. Say the prayer before you go to bed at night.**

Do you ever do things that aren't very nice? Do your Mom or Dad get angry about it? Maybe they might, but you know they still love you, no matter what. They always keep giving you a second chance. That's how it's always been with our loving Father in heaven. Throughout salvation history, God has given his children many chances. One way he gave a second chance to the Israelites was to send them judges.

Gideon was a great judge and a good leader. God spoke to him and told Gideon that he was to save Israel from their enemy, the Midianites (these were the people of Midian).

Gideon asked God for a sign, saying, "I am going to lay a fleece of wool on the threshing floor; if there is dew on the fleece alone, and it is dry on all the ground, then I shall know that you will deliver Israel by my hand, as you have said." The next morning, the fleece was wet and the ground was dry, as Gideon had asked. But Gideon wanted to be doubly sure, so he said to God, "Do not let your anger burn against me…let me, please, make trial with the fleece just once more; let it be dry only on the fleece, and on all the ground let there be dew." And God did just that! Then Gideon trusted God's word and led the people to victory.

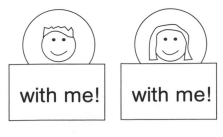

57

God is here

Lord, I know you are with me. Thank you for the gifts you gave me today. I'm sorry for anything bad I did. I want to always be your loving child. Give me your blessing this night. Amen.

Deborah
Judges 4—5

Deborah was a prophetess, but she was also one of Israel's judges. She used to sit under her palm tree and listen to people who came to her for advice. The people knew God was with Deborah and so they would ask her judgment on different matters.

At that time the Canaanite people, led by King Jabin, were very mean to the Israelites. God's people prayed for help against their enemy.

Deborah called Barak to get an army together. She told him God would help him defeat Jabin. Barak said, "I won't go unless you come with me." Deborah left to help him and in the end, King Jabin and the Canaanites were defeated. After that, the Israelites enjoyed peace for forty years.

Below, cut the puzzle triangles and glue them to another piece of paper so they look like this picture. Color it if you wish.

Samson was a priest and a judge of Israel. From the time he was a baby, God intended Samson to one day save Israel from the Philistines. But there was something really special about Samson. God had made him very, very strong. How? By his long hair! In fact, Samson did not need a big army to help him. He was so strong that he could win against 1,000 men. One time in a town called Gaza, he took the gates of the city and their two gate posts, ripped them loose, and carried them on his shoulders!

His girlfriend, Delilah, begged him to tell her why he was so strong. She only wanted to know this because the Philistines had bribed her. Samson told her his secret. Then, while he was sleeping, she had someone shave his head. When he awoke, he was no longer strong. The Philistines took him, made him blind, and threw him into jail. But during his time in prison, his hair grew back.

Then, at one of the Philistines' parties, they brought Samson in to make fun of him in front of everyone. He could not see anything, but he prayed to God. God gave him strength and he pushed the pillars of the building down and crushed all the Philistines. Samson also died that day, but he died a hero.

Samson
Judges 13:1–24; 16:1–31

Unscramble the answers:

1. Who was a priest and judge in this story?
2. What gave him his strength?
3. What group of people did he find victory over?
4. Who had Samson's head shaved?
5. What did Samson knock down at the party?
6. What did Samson do before he took action?

---

1. NOASMS _____

2. SIH NLOG RAIH _____

3. IIHIPLSTSEN _____

4. ALELDIH _____

5. SLILRPA _____

6. EH YARPDE _____

Take a black marker or crayon and draw Samson's long hair.

Ruth
Ruth 1–4

In the time of the judges there lived a couple named Elimelech and Naomi. They had two sons and lived in a place called Moab. When the sons grew up, they each married Moabite women, Orpah and Ruth. Many things happened and in the course of time, Naomi's husband and two sons died.

After that, Naomi decided to go back to the place where she had grown up, to be with her own family. She told her daughters-in-law to go back to their own families, too. Orpah did go, but not Ruth, who said to Naomi, "Wherever you go, I will go; where you lodge, I will lodge; wherever your people shall be my people, and your God my God." And so Ruth went with Naomi to Bethlehem.

When they arrived there, Ruth worked hard in the fields. An important man named Boaz noticed her. He told Ruth, "May the Lord reward you for your deeds...." Boaz soon fell in love with Ruth and married her.

Ruth has a very special role in salvation history. She became the great-grandmother of King David!

Here is a crossword about the story of Ruth.

Down
1. Elimelech married this woman
2. One of Naomi's daughter-in-laws
4. Naomi lived here before she married
7. Boaz told Ruth, "May the Lord _____ you"

Across
3. Ruth was a _____ woman
5. When Naomi's husband and sons died, Naomi returned to her_____
6. Ruth told Naomi, "_____ you go, I will go"
8. This man married Ruth
9. Ruth was great-grandma to this king

You can create your own finger puppet(s) in this activity. Then you can use your finger puppets to act out one of your favorite Old Testament stories!

What you need:

Empty toilet paper roll, paper coffee filter (round and flat, not coned), thick markers, water, eye-dropper, heavy-weight paper plate, small rubber band, plastic craft eyes, hot glue

What to do:

1. Spread newspaper over your workplace. Place one coffee filter on the paper plate. With your thick markers, draw different colors of stripes (leave spaces in between the stripes) across the filter.

2. Take your eye-dropper and place small amounts of water over the filter so that the colors spread. (Don't use too much water.)

3. Let your filter dry completely before lifting it off the plate.

4. Take a rubber band and attach the dry, colored filter to the toilet paper roll, as shown below.

5. Glue on your craft eyes (if you don't have craft eyes, just draw eyes), then make a face on the roll.

6. Look at the contents page in the front of this activity book. Pick a story from November through February. With another friend or a group of friends, act out the story with your puppets.

Make an Israelite

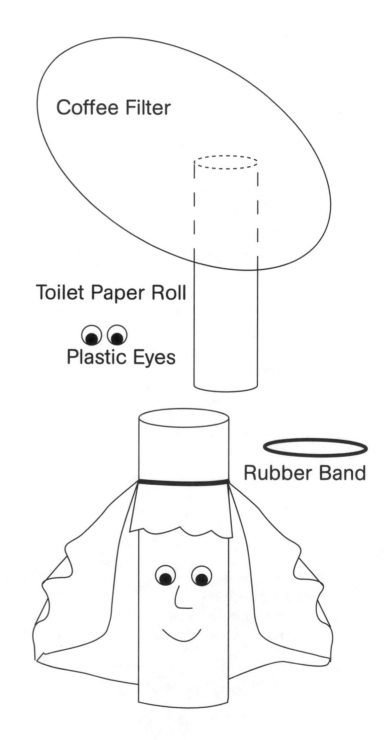

Coffee Filter

Toilet Paper Roll

Plastic Eyes

Rubber Band

March Prayer

Heavenly Father,
All my life you have been so good to me.
You have lavished me with gifts and graces.
I am sorry for the times
I did not show you gratitude.

Forgive me the wrong that I have done
as I forgive others for the times
they hurt me.

Grant that your peace
may always be in my heart.
For this I pray, through Christ, your Son.
Amen

To Parents and Catechists:

Lent is a good opportunity to emphasize to your children the value prayer has in each of our lives. Hannah is known for her earnest prayer; the boy Samuel listened to God's voice and then spoke with God his entire life; David defeated Goliath because he relied on God's help; Solomon's prayer was very pleasing to God. Sometime during this month, you may want to have a brief lenten prayer service in your classroom or home using Psalm 51, David's prayer of contrition. To enhance your prayer time, you can light votive candles, play soft music, and spend a few minutes in silent reflection.

There once lived an Israelite woman named Hannah. She and her husband, Elkanah, did not have any children and Hannah was very sad about that. She prayed to the Lord with great faith, "Lord, look with compassion on me; let me have a son. I promise I will put him at your service as a priest!"

God heard Hannah and gave her a baby son, whom she named Samuel. When he was still a young boy, she brought him to a holy priest named Eli, who raised him in the Lord's service. Every so often, Hannah and Elkanah would visit Samuel and bring their son new clothes to wear. Eli told them, "May God repay you for this gift of your child to him. May you have more children!" In the end, the couple had three more sons and two daughters!

Hannah had faith that God loved her and listened to her prayer. She told everyone what God did for her. You will find Hannah's prayer of praise in the word puzzle below. At the word "Start," draw a line and follow the letters through the maze. You can go up, down, and sideways (but not diagonally). Use each letter only once. Here is her prayer:

Hannah Prays
1 Samuel 1:1–28; 2:18–21

GOD HEARD MY PRAYER AND HE ANSWERED ME!

64

Samuel Is Called

1 Samuel 3:1–10

Here is a fun puzzle. Follow the directions and see if you can find the answer in #3.

1. On the spaces given below each picture, spell out the name of the picture.

— — — — — —   — — — —   — — —   — — —   — — —   — — — —

2. Read the riddles below. You will find the answer to each riddle within the words that you have spelled out above. When you find the answers, cross out only the letters that you need to spell your answer, not the entire word.

- I collect honey and buzz around flowers.

- I am a two-lettered word which people use when they greet each other.

- I am an animal like a moose or a deer and I can be found in colder regions of North America.

- If I am not deaf, I am able to _____.

- I am a round dish and you put cereal in me at break-

3. Write the letters down that you have not crossed out on the lines below. This will spell out another word for a way of life or a calling.

___ ___ ___ ___ ___ ___ ___ ___

One day when Samuel was a little older, the Lord called out to Samuel while he was sleeping. The boy thought it was Eli calling him, and he went to Eli and said, "Here I am." Eli answered, "I didn't call you. Go back to bed."

When Samuel went back to where he had been laying, he heard someone call him again. Once more, Samuel went to Eli. Again, the priest said, "No, I did not call you." Then, for a third time that night, Samuel heard a voice. He got up and said to Eli, "Here I am. You called me." After that Eli knew God was calling Samuel. He told the boy what to do, and so when Samuel heard the voice again, he answered, "Speak, Lord, your servant is listening."

Even though you may not hear God's voice as Samuel did, God will call you to do something special with your life. Whatever you choose to do with your life, be your best at it.

Samuel grew up to be a holy judge and a strong leader of the Israelites. As he aged, the people said, "Some day you will die and what will we do then? We need a good leader. We want a king!" Samuel didn't like that idea. He wanted the people of Israel to look at God as their only king. But Israel wanted to be just like all the other nations around them. They insisted on having a king. So God told Samuel, "Let them have their way. Anoint Saul as their king."

Samuel found Saul and told him of God's plan. He then anointed him with oil as king of the Israelites. But even after Saul was anointed, Samuel knew God had been offended. After all, God had led Israel for so many years. Samuel said, "You want a king to rule over you even though the Lord your God is your king!" Israel was afraid of God's anger. Samuel prayed for them and assured them, saying, "God will not leave you."

Samuel Anoints Saul
1 Samuel 8:1–22; 12:12–25

Look at the pictogram below. Figure out something important that Samuel told the Israelites.

66

Samuel Goes to Jesse's House

1 Samuel 16:1–7

Hold the heart up into the mirror.
Read what God told Samuel.

The Lord does not
see as mortals
see but looks
at the heart.

When God had rejected Saul because of his disobedience, God told Samuel, "Go to Bethlehem where you will find a man named Jesse. You will choose the next king from among his sons."

Samuel did as God asked. When he met Eliah, one of Jesse's sons, he liked the way he looked. Right away he thought, "Surely, this is the son God wants me to anoint." But God thought differently.

With this statement God teaches us not to judge others by how they look. It is who they are that is more important.

Samuel met seven of Jesse's sons but God told him that they were not the ones to be anointed as the future king. Samuel asked if Jesse had any more sons. "Yes," said Jesse. "I have one more. He is the youngest and is out watching the sheep." Samuel said, "Then send for him."

When David came in, God told Samuel, "This is the one you must anoint!" Samuel then got up and took a horn full of oil and anointed David in front of his family.

David remained with his family after he was anointed, until the time that he would be called to serve as king.

David Is Anointed
1 Samuel 16:10–13

Here is a color-by-number for you to do:

1=Red 3=Green 5=Orange 7=Brown
2=Blue 4=Yellow 6=Purple 8=Black

68

David and His Harp

1 Samuel 16:14–23

Find and circle five harps that are hidden in this picture.

Saul had many responsibilities as king, and he had to fight many battles against Israel's enemies. God tried to help Saul but after a while, Saul began to think that his own way of doing things was better than God's. Saul disobeyed God, and so God did not remain with Saul.

Saul grew irritated and moody. His servants heard that a shepherd boy named David knew how to play the harp (Saul did not know that David had been anointed by Samuel to be the next king!). Jesse, David's dad, permitted his son to go and be of service to the king. Whenever Saul felt sad or upset, David would play the harp and soothe the king's spirit.

During the time that Saul was king, the Philistine army came against God's people. This army had a nine foot tall warrior named Goliath, who dared the Israelites, "If any one of you is able to fight with me and kill me, then we will be your servants."

The Israelites were afraid. David, the shepherd boy who played the harp for Saul, went to the king and volunteered to fight Goliath. He told King Saul, "I know God will help me." So David went out before the giant. Goliath laughed when he saw the boy, but David told him, "Today God will give me your life. Then everyone will know there is a God in Israel."

Then David took his slingshot and hurled a stone at the giant's head. Goliath fell down, dead, and David won victory over the Philistines that day.

From this story, we learn that no matter how small or how old someone is, they can do important things. God wants you to feel good about yourself.

After Saul died, David was made king of the Israelites. He ruled for many years, and accomplished great things in his lifetime (although he also did some very bad things). David is said to be the one who wrote the Psalms, which are beautiful song-prayers that can be found in the Bible.

Color and decorate this sign and hang it in your locker or bedroom. Remind yourself how important you are.

David and Goliath
1 Samuel 17:1–48

I LIKE ME!

I like the story of David
And the giant he beat.
The soldiers were afraid,
But David knew no defeat.

He was just a young boy
But he was very smart,
His age didn't matter
With God's trust in his heart.

I am young too;
I know God is with me
And I pray for his help
Every day, faithfully.

I'm not yet full-grown
But I like what I see,
When I look in the mirror and
See who's looking back at me!

King Solomon

I Kings 3:3–15

King Solomon wants to go to Gibeon to pray. But first, help him get a few things before he leaves.

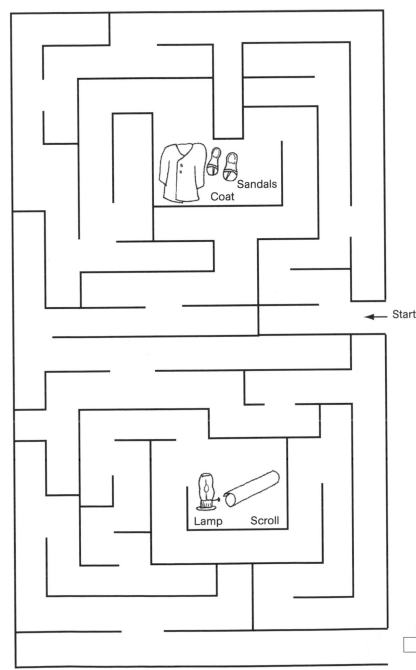

When King David grew old and was about to die, his son, Solomon, was anointed king of Israel.

One day Solomon went to a place called Gibeon. He offered sacrifices to God, who then said to him, "Ask me for whatever you want." Solomon said to God in prayer, "I am a young man and I need to know how to lead your people well. I ask you to teach me how to understand them and to know how to judge between good and evil."

Solomon did not ask for power or money or a long life. Solomon asked for wisdom, and God was very pleased with his prayer. God gave Solomon all that he asked for and more.

71

Prayer

When King Solomon prayed, God heard his prayer. It's important for us to pray, too! You can pray by yourself or with your family. You can pray with your friends or with a whole group of people. No matter where and when you pray, God always listens to you because he loves you.

To the right is a list of different types of prayer. Draw a line to a phrase you might use in each form of prayer. If you are not sure about the answers, ask an adult to help you.

FORM OF PRAYER	In this kind of prayer, you might say
1. ADORATION	A "Please give to me…"
2. THANKSGIVING	B "I adore you my God…"
3. PRAISE	C "I am sorry for my sins…"
4. PETITION	D "Please help someone I know…."
5. CONTRITION	E "Thank you for your gifts…"
6. INTERCESSION	F "I praise you for…"

Sometimes in church the priest burns incense. This is a symbol of our prayers rising to God. Color the shapes below that have an X in them. Leave the other shapes white.

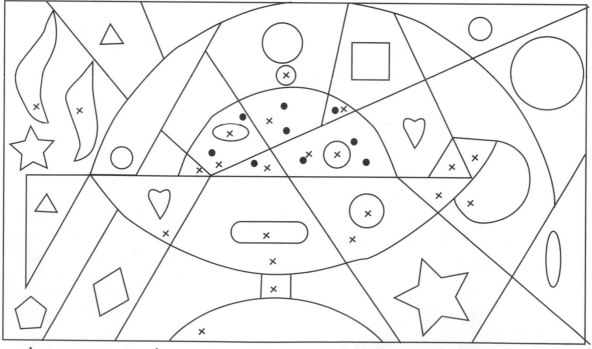

Let my prayer be counted as incense before you. (Psalm 141:2)

April Prayer
Based on Psalm 145

To Parents and Catechists:

The Easter liturgy is all about hope—hope in God who is with us always, who protects us and saves us. April's activity pages speak of people such as Job, Daniel, Jonah, Tobit, and Esther. Each of them had faith and hope that God would deliver them from their trials and each of their stories had a happy ending. Point out to the children that sometimes people we love might not experience a "happy ending" on earth. People who suffer terminal illness or tragic circumstances may only find their happy ending as Christ did, when he rose from the dead in glory after his suffering and death.

(If you wish, have different children or groups take turns praying the verses, while all pray the response.)

Reader I will extol you, O my God and King, and I will bless your name forever and ever.

All I will extol you, O my God and King, and I will bless your name forever and ever.

Reader Jesus, you are the Lamb of God who has taken away the sins of the world.

All I will extol you, O my God and King, and I will bless your name forever and ever.

Reader You loved us and died for us even though we had done nothing for you.

All I will extol you, O my God and King, and I will bless your name forever and ever.

Reader By rising from the grave you gave us hope for eternal life.

All I will extol you, O my God and King, and I will bless your name forever and ever.

Reader Help us to live as your true followers so that we may someday share your glory.

All I will extol you, O my God and King, and I will bless your name forever and ever. Amen.

Job was a very wealthy man who lived in the land of Uz. He had thousands of sheep and cattle and donkeys. He had ten children and many servants. He was a good man who honored and worshiped God.

The devil was wandering the world when he saw God's servant Job. The devil said to God, "Job is faithful to you because he has everything! Take it all away and Job will curse you." God permitted the devil to test Job. Shortly after, Job's children and servants were killed. His animals also died or were stolen. You can imagine how sad Job was! But all he said was, "God gives, God has taken away; blessed be the name of the Lord."

God saw how Job remained faithful even after all that happened to him. Still, the devil persisted: "Take away his health and he will curse you." So God allowed the devil to make Job very sick with painful sores all over his body. Even then, Job said, "We accept happiness from God, shouldn't we also accept pain and sorrow?"

In the end, after Job had suffered a long time, God made Job better again. He gave him back his health and wealth. He gave him ten other children and servants and more animals than he ever had. God rewarded Job for his patience.

Now that you have read this story, fill in the blanks and complete the crossword puzzle.

Job
Job 1—42

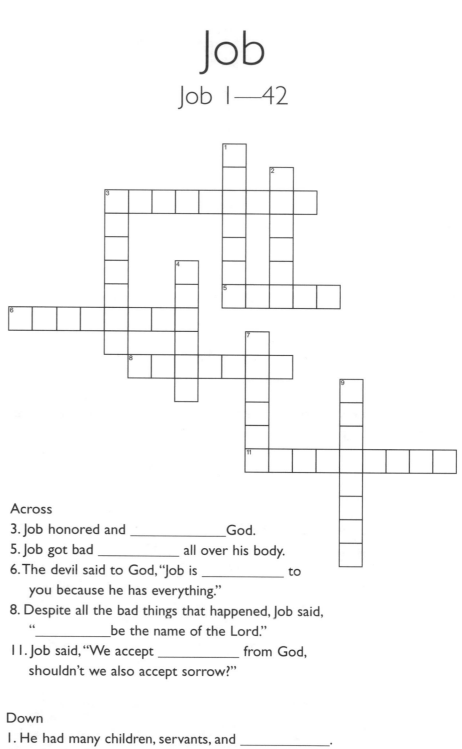

Across

3. Job honored and _____ God.
5. Job got bad _____ all over his body.
6. The devil said to God, "Job is _____ to you because he has everything."
8. Despite all the bad things that happened, Job said, "_____ be the name of the Lord."
11. Job said, "We accept _____ from God, shouldn't we also accept sorrow?"

Down

1. He had many children, servants, and _____.
2. God made Job _____ again.
3. Job was a very _____ man.
4. Job's children and servants were _____.
7. God allowed the devil to take away Job's good _____.
9. God rewarded Job for his _____.

74

Daniel and the Lions
Daniel 6:1–29

Below, help Daniel get through the maze safely.

Start ↓

Exit

Daniel, help me trust in God as you did!

When Darius was king of Babylon, he chose a man named Daniel as one of three administrators. The other two were jealous of Daniel and they wanted to get rid of him. They noticed how Daniel prayed to God three times a day. They told the king, "No one should pray to any god but you. If they do, let them be thrown to the lions."

Darius thought that sounded like a good idea, so he made it a law. Daniel didn't care about the new law. He knew that he should praise and honor the one, true God no matter what, so he continued to pray.

Darius liked Daniel a lot. When the two jealous administrators told him about Daniel's prayers, Darius regretted making the new law. But he felt that he had to carry out the punishment, and Daniel was thrown into a den of ferocious lions. Darius told Daniel, "May your God save you from the lions."

The next morning King Darius ran to the lions' den and saw that Daniel had not been harmed. Daniel was surely a man of great faith!

Long ago, there was a big city called Nineveh. God was angry at the people of Nineveh because they were wicked. God spoke to a man named Jonah and said to him, "Go to Nineveh, and tell the people there that they must change their ways."

Jonah was scared. He didn't want to do this and so he tried to hide from God. He went on board a ship going in the opposite direction of Nineveh. But during a bad storm, Jonah was thrown overboard, and he was swallowed by a large fish.

For three days and nights Jonah was in the belly of that fish. While he was there, Jonah realized he couldn't run away from God, and so he prayed to God for help. God told the big fish to throw Jonah up onto dry land. Then Jonah went to Nineveh and preached God's message. He told the people that they must show they were sorry for their wicked ways. In the end, the people listened to Jonah and did what God wanted, and God forgave them.

Jonah
Jonah 1—3

Find and circle the three identical whales.

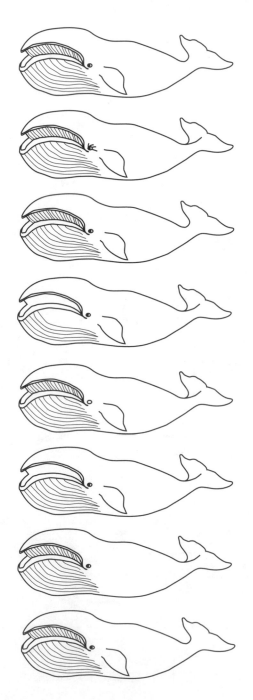

Isaiah

Isaiah 6:1–8

Cross out letters S through Z:

T Y H U S E Z W R X V E   __ __ __ __

Cross out letters N through V:

O U I N V Q A R T M P S   __ __ __ __

Cross out letters F through M:

M H S F K G E I N J L D G   __ __ __ __

Cross out letters A through D:

C A M D B E A C!   __ __!

Make up a five to ten sentence story about one of the children below. Each of them was called by God to do something special for someone else. Give each of the children a name and tell what special thing he or she did.

Isaiah was a very holy man. Because of this God showed himself to Isaiah. When Isaiah saw how beautiful God was, he adored God. He was so happy, but at the same time he felt sad because he knew how unworthy he was in God's presence. So an angel came and touched Isaiah's lips and said, "Your sins are forgiven."

God needed a prophet, a special messenger to God's people, and so God said to Isaiah, "Whom shall I send…who will go for us?" Being a prophet was not an easy job. Sometimes the people of God were stubborn and wouldn't listen. But Isaiah didn't run away from God. He answered God.

What did Isaiah say to God? Cross out the letters as instructed. Write the letters that are left on the lines.

God knows it isn't always easy being kind and helpful especially when it means giving up something you want to do. At those moments, whisper Isaiah's prayer and do it anyway. It will make you feel good about yourself. Most important, God will notice every bit of your generosity and will reward you!

What do you know about prophets? See if you can finish these sentences on your own. Use the words in the box to fill in the blanks.

Messiah	pleased
punish	message
prophets	books
reward	female

PROPHET NAME SEARCH

There were many prophets throughout salvation history. Here are just some of the names of prophets who came before Jesus was born. Find these in the Name Search below. (Deborah and Huldah were female prophets or "prophetesses.")

Prophet Trivia

1. A prophet is someone sent by God to give a _____ to God's people.

2. Sometimes, the prophet tells the people that God is _____ with them and will _____ them for their faithfulness.

3. At other times, the prophet also tells them when they are doing wrong and that God will _____ them if they do not repent of their sin.

4. Some prophets spoke about the Savior, or _____, who would come some day.

5. A prophetess is a _____ prophet.

6. There are eighteen _____ of the _____ in the Old Testament.

H A R O B E D N H F
A J M L J P D H A S
I J O O N O A S D A
M O S R S J N D L M
E E E G I K I A U U
R L S L Q B E G H E
E Z E K I E L Y C L
J P M A H S I L E F
I S A I A H O S E A

Amos	Elisha	Huldah	Jonah
Daniel	Ezekiel	Isaiah	Moses
Deborah	Gad	Jeremiah	Samuel
Elijah	Hosea	Joel	

Tobit

Tobit 1—14

In this, each letter follows a different pattern of raised dots so the blind person can "feel" the words with his or her hand. Here is the Braille alphabet. Use it to decipher something Tobit said.

A B C D E F G H I J K L M

N O P Q R S T U V W X Y Z

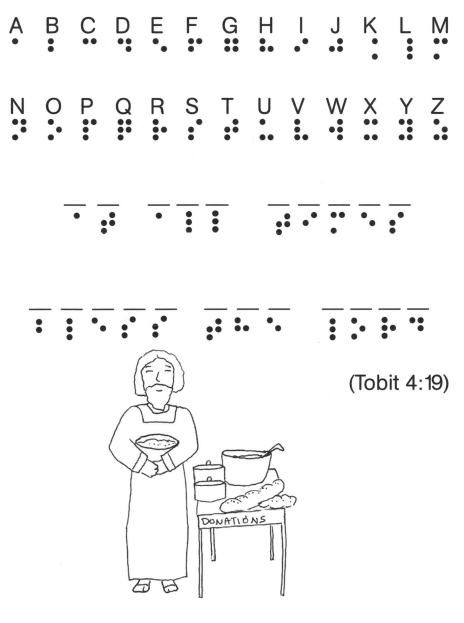

(Tobit 4:19)

Tobit was a gentle man who loved God and followed the law of Israel. Every so often he traveled to Jerusalem and gave donations to the priests, the poor, and the widows. Everyone knew that Tobit had great respect for the dead. In fact he would bury the dead bodies of his countrymen, even if they weren't his relatives.

God was very happy with Tobit, but God wanted to test him. God let Tobit become blind. Yet Tobit remained faithful to God, even though being blind was a terrible suffering for him.

A disguised angel named Raphael was sent to Tobit to help his family. Four years after Tobit became blind, Raphael restored his sight. In the end, Raphael revealed who he was and told Tobit, "God is very pleased with you!"

Did you ever hear of Louis Braille? He was a French teacher who lived in the early 1800s who thought of a way to help blind people read. He invented the Braille system.

In Persia long ago, there lived a beautiful Jewish girl named Esther. Her parents had died and her cousin, Mordecai, adopted her and raised her. At that time, Ahasuerus, the king of Persia, was looking for a wife. Many young girls went before him, but he thought Esther was the most beautiful of them all. So the king chose her as his queen.

The king had a top officer named Haman who didn't like Mordecai. Haman found out that Mordecai was a Jew and so he ordered all the Jews to be killed. Mordecai then told Esther to go to the king and tell him about Haman's plot.

At that time, no one was allowed to enter the king's presence unless they were called—not even the queen. But Esther prayed to God, and she received the courage to go to the king. He told her, "I will give you anything you want." Esther asked that her life be spared, along with all the Jewish people. The king couldn't believe his ears! He hadn't known Esther was Jewish, and to think Haman would have murdered her too! In the end, the king had Haman killed. All the Jewish people were saved because of Esther's faith and courage.

Esther
Esther 2—8

Find the crown that matches Queen Esther's. Then color the king and queen.

Important Places in the Old Testament

In this activity, you will find and write down the names of important places that you have read about in some of the stories from the Old Testament.

Read one sentence at a time. Each one names an important place. Find that place on the map, then write the name of that place on the line after the sentence. If you need help remembering the names of these places, you can look up the stories by using the page numbers given after each sentence.

MEDITERRANEAN SEA

CANAAN ②

⑦ Jericho

⑨ Jerusalem

⑧ Bethlehem

❸ EGYPT

Mt. Sinai ⑥

❹ Midian

❺ RED SEA

⑩ Nineveh

❶ Ur

PERSIAN GULF

1. Abraham was living in this town when God called him. ———————————————— p.27
2. God brought Abraham to this land, where he settled. It was later known as the "Promised Land."
   ———————————————— p.55
3. The Israelites became slaves here under a very mean Pharaoh. —————————— p.36
4. Moses worked as a shepherd and saw the burning bush here. —————————— p.37
5. When Moses led the Israelites out of Egypt, God parted these waters so they could cross.
   ———————————————— p.41
6. God gave Moses the Ten Commandments on this mountain. ——————————————— p.44
7. All the walls fell down in this place after Joshua led the people in battle here. ————————— p.55
8. Ruth and Naomi went here after their husbands died. Many years later, Jesus was born here.
   ———————————————— p.61
9. This place was known as the City of David ————————————— p.89
10. This is the place where Jonah was sent to preach. ————————————— p.76

May Prayer

To Parents and Catechists:

As we draw near to the end of the school year, we will summarize important messages given throughout salvation history. Activities for May point out the value of prayer, of vocation, of living a good life, and of remembering that God is always with us, just as God was with our ancestors. The page "God Is with Us" hints of the fulfillment of God's promise found in Christ's coming.

Blessed Mother Mary,

In baptism God called me

to be someone special.

God called me to love and to serve him.

I know that every breath I take

is a gift from God

And every moment I live

should be given back to God.

Help me, then,

from this day forward

to always be God's loving child.

Amen.

Elijah and the Widow

1 Kings 16:29–34; 17:1–24

Imagine that you are the widow from the story above. A news reporter from the Zarephath Tribune newspaper comes to your house to interview you. How would you answer the reporter's questions? (Read 1 Kings 17:8–24 for details about this story.)

1. How did you feel when Elijah the prophet asked you for the last bit of your bread?

2. Were you surprised to find the jars full even after you took flour and oil from them?

3. What made you think that Elijah was really a man of God?

4. When your son died, what did you say to Elijah?

5. What happened after you spoke to Elijah?

6. How did it make you feel when you saw your son alive and well again?

After Solomon died, other kings ruled Israel but they were not always faithful to God. They worshiped false gods and brought God's anger upon the people. During one of these times, God sent a prophet named Elijah to the people. Because there was a drought in the land (a drought is when it doesn't rain for a long, long time), Elijah had no water to drink. God told him to go to a town named Zarephath, and "A widow there will feed you."

When Elijah came to Zarephath, he met a widow and said, "Bring me water and some bread as well." The widow replied, "I am going to bake some bread and then I will be out of flour and oil." Elijah said, "Bake me bread and God will take care of you." The woman did as the prophet asked and he was right. The woman's jars of flour and oil never ran empty!

While Elijah was at her house, the lady's son died. Elijah prayed for him, and the son was raised to life again. The widow said, "I know now that you are truly a man of God!"

God Speaks to Elijah
I Kings 19:1–18

Long ago, during the time of the prophet Elijah, a very bad king named Ahab ruled over Samaria. He and his wife Jezebel had commanded the people to worship false gods, and so God sent prophets to stop this practice. Elijah was one of those prophets. He proved to the people just how phony the false gods were! That made the king and queen very upset, and they tried to find Elijah and kill him.

Elijah ran away from the city as fast as he could! He traveled forty days straight until he reached Mount Horeb, where he slept in a cave. There the word of Yahweh came to him: "Go out and stand on the mountain, for God is passing by." A hurricane came, but God was not in the hurricane. Then an earthquake came, and fire, but God was not in them either. Then a light whispering sound came and Elijah covered his face because he knew God was there.

Use the words in the box to finish the sentences.

HOREB	HURRICANE	AHAB	EARTHQUAKE
JEZEBEL	WHISPER	FIRE	PROPHET

1. King_____ and Queen_____ led the people to believe in false gods.
2. Elijah was a great _____.
3. When the king and queen were trying to kill Elijah, he fled to Mount _____.
4. God was not in the _____ or the _____ or the _____.
5. Elijah knew God passed by when he heard a _____.

Find the letters W H I S P E R in the drawing below.

84

Naaman Is Cured

2 Kings 5:1–19

Elisha was another great prophet. People believed he had some of Elijah's spirit in him. One time an important officer named Naaman, from the Assyrian army, traveled many miles to see Elisha. Naaman had leprosy, and he was hoping Elisha would cure him.

Elisha told Naaman to wash in the Jordan River seven times. At first Naaman was angry that he had come a great distance just to have the prophet tell him to bathe in the river. But Naaman's servants told him that he should do as Elisha said. Finally, Naaman did and his leprosy was cured. After that, Naaman believed in the God of Israel and promised to serve God always.

Naaman thought he would have to do something extraordinary in order to get cured. But he didn't. God just wanted to see his willingness to obey. When he did what he was supposed to do, God cured him.

Just like Naaman, God can work wonders for each of us—we just have to be willing to do the small things that come our way. It's OK to do big things, too, but sometimes it's the little things that are the hardest to do.

Circle the little things that God would be pleased to see you do during the day.

HOLD THE DOOR FOR SOMEONE	STAR ON A TV SHOW
BUILD A TALL SKYSCRAPER	WIN A WORLD CHAMPIONSHIP
HELP WITH THE DISHES	CLIMB A MOUNTAIN
OBEY YOUR PARENTS AND TEACHERS	PRAISE A FRIEND
FEED YOUR PET	TRY NOT TO ARGUE WITH YOUR BROTHER OR SISTER

Connect the dots and draw a happy face on Naaman.

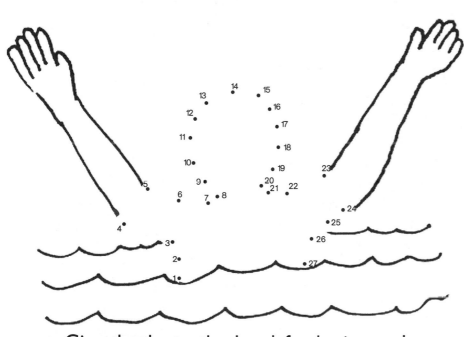

Give thanks to the Lord, for he is good;
his steadfast love endures forever! Psalm 118:1

The Psalms

In the Bible there is a collection of prayer songs, called psalms, that were written in Old Testament times. Many of these were written by King David. The psalms have been a popular way to pray throughout our history, from ancient times to now—even Jesus used the psalms!

The psalms are almost like a telephone call to God. When we want to talk to one of our friends we might pick up the phone and call them. When we want to talk with God, we can pick up the Bible and open it to the Book of Psalms. After you are done reading, talk to God about anything that is in your heart.

As a prayerful activity, open your Bible to the Book of Psalms. Think about being in God's presence. Turn to each psalm listed and read it slowly, taking time to think about the words.

At what part of the Mass do we say or sing a psalm? Circle your answer:

A. After the Gospel

B. After the First Reading

C. After Communion

Spend quality time with the Lord. What kind of psalm in the right column best describes a psalm in the left column? Write the letter in the box.

A. Psalm 23   ☐ ...about sorrow for sin

B. Psalm 51   ☐ ...about thanksgiving

C. Psalm 63   ☐ ...about God being our shepherd

D. Psalm 138   ☐ ...about longing for God

Be filled with the Spirit, as you sing psalms and hymns and spiritual songs, singing and making melody to the Lord in your hearts. (Ephesians 5:18–19)

Make a Fortune!

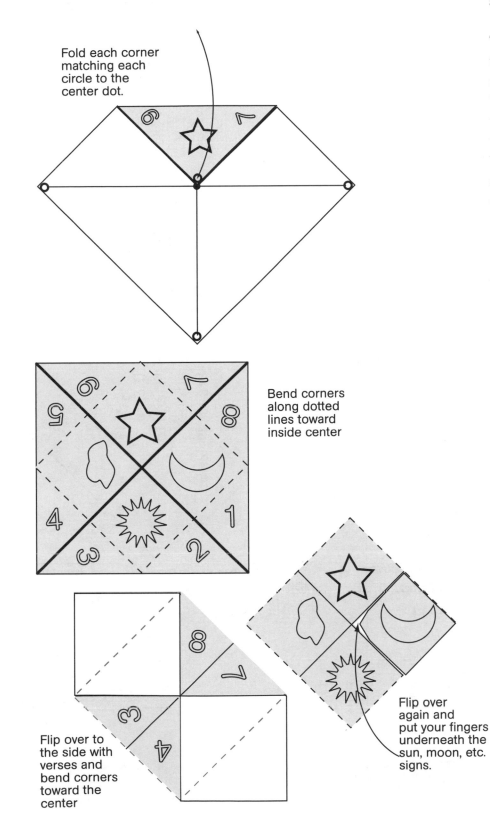

Fold each corner matching each circle to the center dot.

Bend corners along dotted lines toward inside center

Flip over to the side with verses and bend corners toward the center

Flip over again and put your fingers underneath the sun, moon, etc. signs.

The Book of Proverbs gives us many useful hints about how to think, talk, act, live, and love the Lord.

Have you ever made a "fortune"? This is a piece of paper that you fold then move with your fingers to tell messages just for fun. Make this "fortune" and use it to tell proverbs to your friends. Follow all the directions in order.

What you need:

scissors, glue, and crayons or markers, and access to a photocopier.

1. Photocopy the next page and cut along the lines that say "cut."

2. Fold the photocopy in half corner to corner, then side to side.

3. On the blank side, fold the pointed edges toward the center (axis of creases) so all four corners meet in the middle.

4. Turn this square over. Fold the corner edges toward the center so that all you see are the numbered corners,

5. Flip over so that all you see are the stars, moon, clouds, and sun symbols. Put your fingers underneath the flaps of the symbols and pop the flaps to force the symbols together to make a square.

6. With a pulling and pushing motion, make the fortune go back and forth. Tell a friend to choose a picture. With each movement, spell out the word. Then have him/her choose a number. Count out the number as you move your fingers. Tell them to choose another number. Lift the flap to read the proverb your friend chose.

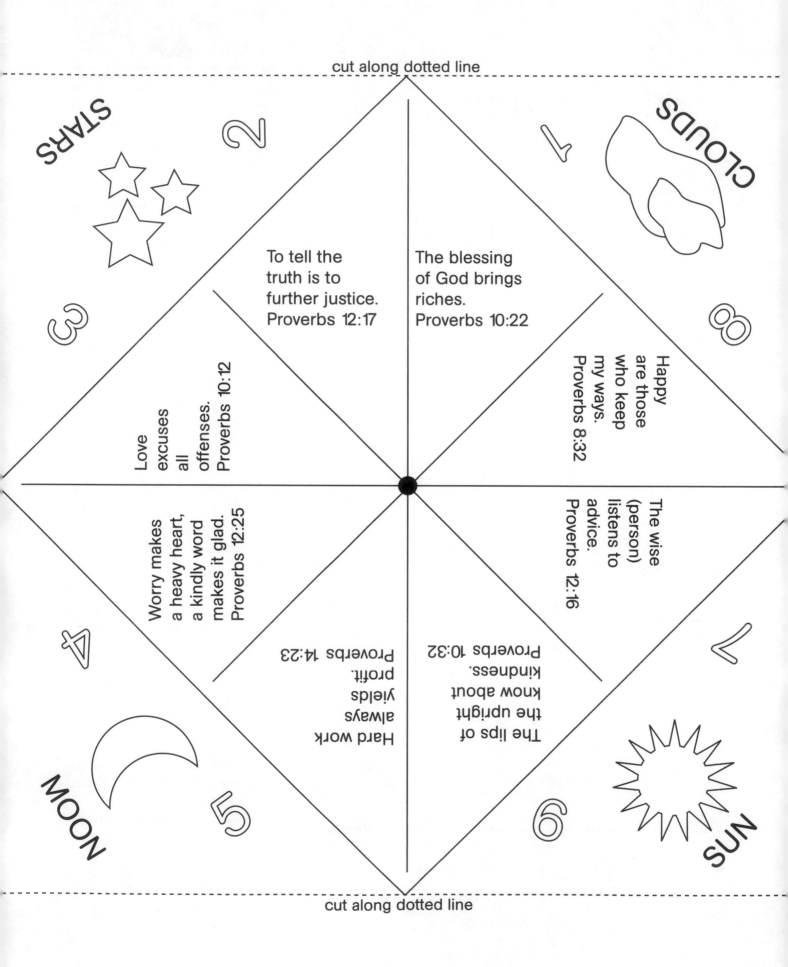

cut along dotted line

STARS

2

CLOUDS

1

To tell the truth is to further justice. Proverbs 12:17

The blessing of God brings riches. Proverbs 10:22

3

8

Happy are those who keep my ways. Proverbs 8:32

Love excuses all offenses. Proverbs 10:12

Worry makes a heavy heart, a kindly word makes it glad. Proverbs 12:25

The wise (person) listens to advice. Proverbs 12:16

4

7

Hard work always yields profit. Proverbs 14:23

The lips of the upright know about kindness. Proverbs 10:32

MOON

5

6

SUN

cut along dotted line

God Is with Us
Jeremiah 39:1–10; 52:1–30; Ezra 1–6

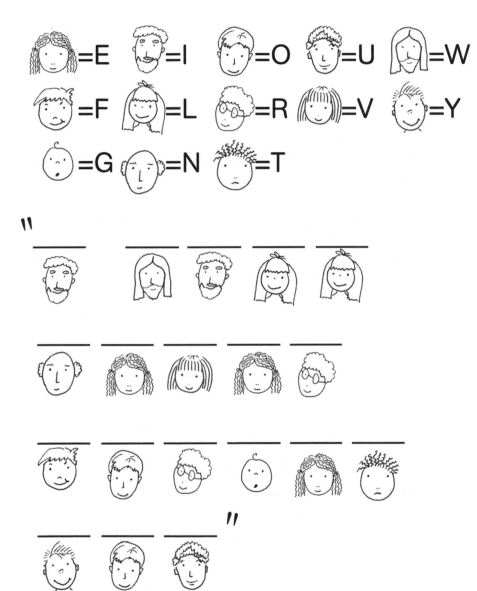

About 600 years before Jesus was born, there lived a king named Nebuchadnezzar. He came with all his soldiers to Jerusalem, burned the city, and took the Jewish people captive to a land called Babylon. It was very hard for the Hebrews to leave their homeland.

During those years, important prophets like Jeremiah and Ezekiel encouraged the people to remain faithful and to obey God's commandments. Many years later, King Cyrus let the Jewish people return to Jerusalem and rebuild a beautiful temple.

Throughout salvation history, God has been like a father and a mother to his people. God protects us today as he protected our ancestors. God is with us, and tells us over and over again about how important we are to him. As proof of this great love, God sent us his only son, Jesus.

In Isaiah 49:15, God asks us, "Can a mother ever forget her tiny baby?" Then God tells us even more. Use the pictogram to find the answer.

God wants you to always remember how much you are loved.

What you need:
Scissors, a pen or pencil, glue, two small magnets, and clear contact paper or tape (optional).

Refrigerator Reminder of God's Love for Us

Write your name on the line in the first hand, under the word "Dear." Now write the the name of someone special on the second hand. Cut out the circles and cover them with clear contact paper or tape if you want to strengthen the paper. (Or you can glue the circle on to a piece of heavy paper or cardboard.) Then glue a small magnet onto the back of each circle. Now you have a refrigerator reminder magnet for yourself and someone you love.

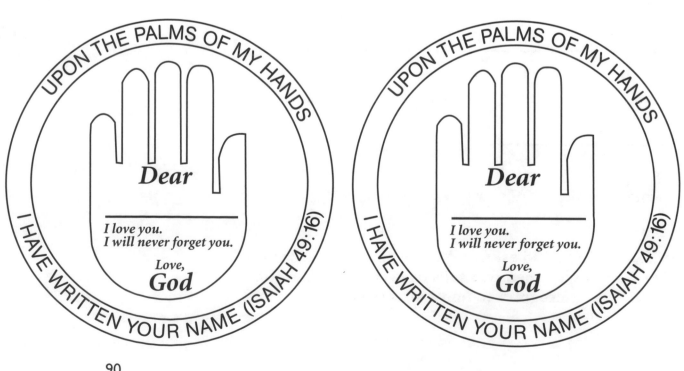

End of School Year

Jesus,

I pray that you bless all the people

who helped me learn something

this year.

Bless my family and friends,

and help everyone to have

a safe and happy summer.

Make me remember that

you are with me

and remind me to tell you every day

that I love you. Amen.

Answer Pages

September

God's Letter to us: Pictures going down are: Book, Igloo, Bell, Lamb, Eye. Letters in squares spell out BIBLE.

A Treasure for You: Answers to Clues going down spell out: GODS WORD. Bible should be circled.

The Word of God:

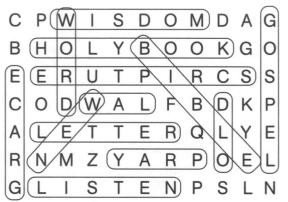

Finding Your Way in the Bible: #2: There are FOUR chapters in the Book of Ruth.

#5: Melchizadek brought out BREAD and WINE.

#6: The names of Noah's sons are SHEM, HAM and JAPHETH.

God Guides Us: Cryptoquip reads, "Your Word is a lamp for my feet, a light on my path."

Creature Feature

October

Creation: Things Adam and Eve may have seen in the garden: Moon, Tree, Snake, Flower, Apple, Butterfly, Sun, Bird, Star

Adam and Eve: Pictograph reads: "God sees everything!"

A Promised Savior: Mystery picture in the graph is of the Blessed Mother and baby Jesus.

Cain and Abel: Turned upside down, the drawing of the boy looks like a monster:

Noah: God told Noah, "That is the sign of the covenant I have established between myself and all living things on earth." Unscrambled letters read, "The rainbow."

November

God Calls Abram: There are 13 six-pointed stars.

Abraham and Sarah: Cryptoquip reads, "Nothing is impossible with God."

Isaac:

Mirror sign reads, Jesus "Behold the Lamb of God" (Jn 1:29)

Jacob: Things to circle: celery, carrots, onions, tomatoes, peas, potatoes, corn, salt, meat.

Jacob's Sons: Town in Mt 2:6: BETHLEHEM. JESUS was born there.

Joseph's Colorful Coat: First column, third coat has three buttons.

December

Baby Moses: Objects circled are; Rattle, Blanket, Doll. Message in the basket reads, "Before I formed you in the womb I knew you."

Moses is Called:

MOSES
PHARAOH
HEBREWS
SLAVES
MIDIAN
SHEPHERD
BUSH
FIRE
GOD
EGYPT
FREE
CANAAN

Pharaoh is Stubborn: Cryptoquip reads, "Let my people go!" Dot-to-dot is a snake.

The Ten Plagues: Hidden expression to Pharaoh: "Obey the Lord!"

The First Passover: Matching Pharaoh is bottom center.

Parting of the Red Sea:

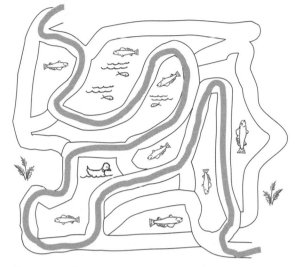

The Pentateuch:

Possible three-lettered words: Cat, pat, hat, hen, pen, ten, nut, hut, cut, put, tan, pan, can, eat, ate, tea, the, pet, net, tap, cap, nap, act, cup, cue, ant, pun

Possible four-lettered words: Tent, chat, teen, heat, peat, neat, tape, etch, path, punt, hunt, hate, chap, cute, each, cane, heap, that, pent, pant, tact, cent, taut, tune, puce, pace, hath, cape, ache, nape, tact, tuna, pact, then

Possible five-lettered words: Peach, teach, peace, cheap, cheep, cheat, taunt, haunt, chant, teeth, chute, patch, punch, acute, enact, heath, tenet

January

The Ten Commandments: Math answers from top to bottom: 6 =A; 2=C; 3=D; 1=U; 4=L; 7=E; 5=O; 8=G Another name for the Ten Commandments is "The Decalogue."

Names of God: "I Am Who I Am"; "Yahweh"

Food From Heaven:

Pictures top half are: comb, car, hand, phone, cat. Hidden word: Manna

Pictures bottom half are: owl, baby, star, bell, cross. Hidden word: Water

Children in the Desert: Ben got the wood for the fire, Anna gathered reeds to make a basket, Rachel cleaned pots by the stream, Josh collected stones to put around the campfire, Judith brought fresh water from the spring.

What is a Covenant?:

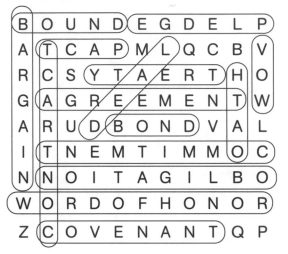

The Ark of the Covenant: The Ten Commandments were kept inside the Ark of the Covenant.

The Israelites Grumble: There are twelve spies. The Israelites wandered in the desert for FORTY YEARS.

February

The Walls of Jericho: Message in the Wall reads, "I will always be with you; I will never leave you."

Joshua: Answers to the clues from top to bottom: hot, meals, hens, safe, heel, low, drive, drum, dry, wool. Joshua's saying is, "As for me and my household we will serve the Lord."

Samson: Answers: Samson; His long hair; Philistines; Delilah; Pillars; He prayed.

Ruth:

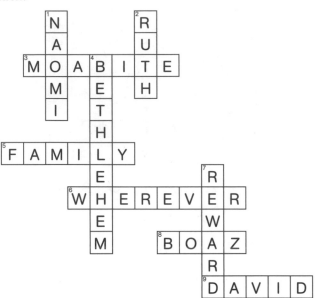

March

Hannah Prays:

Samuel is Called: #1: beehive, lock, hat, ear, bow, lion. #2: bee, hi, elk, hear, bowl

#3 vocation

Samuel Anoints Saul: Pictogram reads, "You must worship the Lord with all of your heart."

David and His Harp:

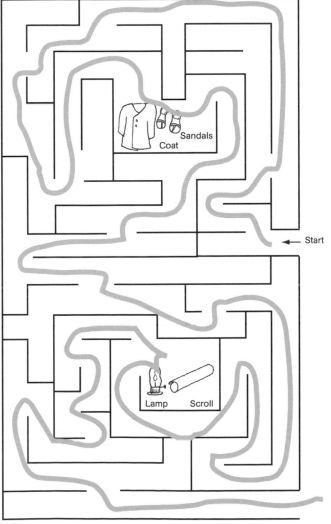

King Solomon:

Sandals
Coat

Lamp   Scroll

Start

Prayer: Forms of prayer: 1=B, 2=E, 3=F, 4=A, 5=C, 6=D. Hidden picture is incense lamp.

April
Job:

Daniel and the Lions:

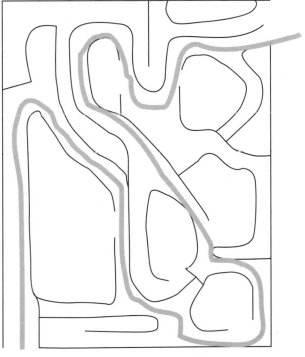

Jonah: The 1st, 3rd and 8th whales match.

Isaiah: Words of Isaiah: "Here I am send me!"

Prophet Trivia: 1. message, 2. pleased/reward, 3. punish, 4. messiah, 5. female, 6. books/prophets

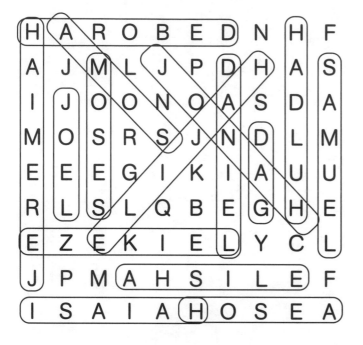

Tobit: Braille message of Tobit reads: "At all times bless the Lord."

Esther: Second crown in the second column.

Important Places: #1 Ur; #2 Canaan; #3 Egypt; #4 Midian; #5 Red Sea; #6 Mt. Sinai; #7 Jericho; #8 Bethlehem; #9 Jerusalem; #10 Nineveh

May

God Speaks to Elijah: #1 King Ahab and Queen Jezebel; #2 prophet; #3 Horeb; #4 hurricane, earthquake, fire; #5 whisper

Naaman is Cured: Phrases circled: Hold the door for someone; Help with the dishes; Try not to argue with your brother or sister; Obey your parents and teachers; Feed your pet; Praise a friend.

The Psalms: We say or sing a Psalm AFTER THE FIRST READING A=3rd, B=1st, C=4th, D=2nd

God is With Us: Pictogram reads, "I will never forget you."

Of Related Interest

My Favorite Jesus Activity Book

Jenny Erickson

From mazes to crossword puzzles, from connect the dots to calendars, there are over 60 pages of tried and tested fun activities to reproduce and use with youngersters from preschool on up. 1-58595-200-1, 112 pp, $14.95 (X-38)

Jesus & Mary in the Rosary

Echo Stories for Children
Learners Mimic the Words and Actions of the Storyteller
Page McKean Zyromski

Helps catechists teach children the main events in the lives of Jesus and Mary as described in the mysteries of the Rosary.

1-58595-140-4, 144 pp, $19.95 (J-87)

Echo Stories for Children

Celebrating Saints and Seasons in Word and Action
Page McKean Zyromski

These 20 delightful stories involve children in the "telling" voice and body and students imitate and mirror the teacher's voice and actions.

0-89622-930-0, 168 pp, $19.95 (B-76)

The Complete Children's Liturgy Book

Liturgies of the Word for Years A, B, C
Katie Thompson

Attractively illustrated, this book offers a complete but flexible scheme for celebrating the Liturgy of the Word with children for every Sunday and major feast days. 0-89622-695-6, 352 pp, $39.95 (M-70)

100 Creative Teaching Techniques for Religion Teachers

Phyllis vos Wezeman

A wealth of practical possibilities for telling and reviewing the stories of Scripture and faith to their classes. 1-58595-141-2, 112 pp, $12.95 (J-89)

TWENTY-THIRD PUBLICATIONS

185 WILLOW STREET • PO BOX 180 • MYSTIC, CT 06355
TEL: 1-800-321-0411 • FAX: 1-800-572-0788
Bayard   E-MAIL: ttpubs@aol.com • www.twentythirdpublications.com